D1565401

PROFANE PLAY,

RITUAL,

AND

JEAN GENET

PROFANE PLAY, RITUAL, AND JEAN GENET

A Study of His Drama

by
Lewis T. Cetta

Studies In The Humanities
Literature

The University of Alabama Press
University, Alabama

Copyright © 1974
By The University of Alabama Press
ISBN 0–8173–7313–6
Library of Congress Catalog Card Number 73–10651

 **PREFACE**

The preface to a book of this sort usually consists of a series of *pro forma* acknowledgments that the author makes to some of those who have aided him. The acknowledgments listed herein, however, are not meant to be *pro forma*. If they seem so, it may be laid to an awkwardness on my part, not to a lack of felicity or generosity in those who are listed. No *pro forma* acknowledgment, for instance, can express my deep and abiding appreciation to Professor William Wasserstrom of Syracuse University, who inspired the present book. Nor can it state my profound indebtedness to him for his earnest encouragement and for his numerous helpful suggestions.

To Professor Sidney Thomas I owe a debt of gratitude for his help, his understanding, and his patient consideration.

The book would have proven a more difficult task without the aid of Mr. and Mrs. Gurdip Sethi, who suggested sources in Sanskrit drama and etymology without which the chapter on *The Blacks* would seem incomplete. And to Miss Judith Schmidt of Grove Press, Inc., too, who arranged a private showing of Genet's film *Chant d'amour* for me, I owe thanks.

Finally, to Mr. and Mrs. Paul Veillette, I owe thanks for their offer of a "holiday haven" in the country, where I could put my thoughts in shape without interruption.

L. T. C.

CONTENTS

PROFANE PLAY,

RITUAL,

AND

JEAN GENET

 **INTRODUCTION**

In many critical works, the author begins each chapter with a brief telling passage, either a self-revealing quotation from one of his subject's works or a perceptive insight into the subject's major themes by another critic. This work, however, opens not with a quotation, but with a symbol—the Taoist cosmological symbol for *yang* and *yin*. It seems, at first, rather strange, I suppose, to begin a work on Jean Genet, a twentieth-century French author, with a symbol drawn from the pre-Christian Orient. And yet, if a theatrical director were to stage Genet's *The Balcony*, *The Blacks*, or *The Screens*, he could do no better than to incorporate into the stage setting a slowly revolving *yang-yin* symbol, for it would not be an extraneous importation imposed upon the fabric of these dramas, but rather an integrated pictograph of almost every major theme that the dramas contain. Moreover, if we believe that there are any implications at all for modern humanity to be found in the present era's conclusions from investigations into primitive societies and ancient civilizations (such as Carl Jung's concept of the *collective unconscious*), then it becomes relatively easy to accept the Taoist symbol as expressive of Genet's world view.

When the polarities inherent in any Genet drama and the dialectic between them are pondered, then the convenient use of Taoism to explain them becomes even more apparent. *Yang*, the male principle, and *yin*, the female principle, sum up all of life's polarities: good (*yang*)-evil (*yin*), dynamic-static, day-night, sun-moon, positive-negative. These attributes, however, are not diametrically opposed; for, in looking at the symbol, we find that not only does each principle complement the other, but it also locates itself in the other's territory. And both are contained within the all-embracing, infinitely revolving circle so that seeming opposites become phases of the revolving ring. Like life itself, the figure does not move onward in a continuum toward a fixed goal. Rather it signifies that all things come full circle and that, at center, all things are one.

Genet's drama, if it deals with anything at all, presents primarily a study of polarities. Particularly evident in the dramas is the interplay of good and evil and of reality and illusion. One is struck, for example, by Genet's handling of illusion and reality. All of his dramatic works deal in some fashion with characters who are caught in the reality-oriented world and who act out their fantasies in masquerade, impersonation, and play-acting. They all deal, too, with the interaction between good and evil. In fact, in the seemingly topsy-turvy world that Genet creates on the stage, two opposing attributes such as good and evil or reality and illusion appear to exchange places and, at times, to merge into one another in a nightmarish and hallucinatory fashion. And throughout all his dramatic *oeuvre* stands the symbol of the mirror, image of that world of illusion that preoccupies him. There is no doubt that, had Genet lived in a previous era in Western Society, he, like the Marquis de Sade, would have been in a madhouse because of his artistic vision.

Perhaps, however, the single most prominent feature of Genet's drama is the fashion in which he elucidates his study of opposites through the use of games and play. For example, in the drama *Deathwatch* (*Haute Surveillance*), the character Lefranc plays at being a real "tough" like Green Eyes or Snowball; Claire and Solange, the two maids in *The Maids* (*Les Bonnes*), play at being their mistress; clients of the bordello in *The Balcony* (*Le Balcon*) play sexual games of masquerade with the prostitutes; masked blacks in *The Blacks* (*Les Nègres*) play at being powerful whites; and various characters such as the Mother and Leïla in *The Screens* (*Les Paravents*) play at being barnyard animals. Completely inescapable, then, is the conclusion that, in Genet, the theme of play is utterly bound up with the themes of illusion and reality and of good and evil. Yet, curiously, no comprehensive study of Genet's use of play in his dramas has ever appeared. It will be the purpose of this book to unravel some of the uses that Genet makes of play and to investigate its connection with illusion and evil.

Genet has decided for illusion over reality just as he has chosen evil over good, homosexuality over heterosexuality, and death over life. But Genet's choices and preferences should come as no great surprise to the reader; for the nature of illusion is such that anyone who would call himself an artist must engage himself in it to a greater or lesser degree whenever it becomes apparent to him that he cannot operate within the framework of a society in which what Freud terms the "reality principle" is an overpowering force. The artist's immersion in the creative process is, according to Freud, a "sublimation of the instincts" in order to shift the instinctual aims in such a manner that they cannot be frustrated by the external world. The creative process, is, consequently, *inner-oriented:*

> the connection with reality is . . . loosened; *satisfaction is obtained from illusions* [Italics mine], which are recognized as such without the discrepancy between them and reality being allowed to interfere with enjoyment. The regions from which these illusions arise is the life of the imagination; at the time when the development of the sense of reality took place, this region was expressly exempted from the demands of reality-testing and was set apart for the purpose of fulfilling wishes which were difficult to carry out. At the head of these satisfactions through phantasy stands the enjoyment of works of art. [1]

Illusion and dream, according to Freud, share a common ground in that both are often forms of wish-fulfillment and both spring from the primordial regions of the unconscious, albeit often in disguised form. They, therefore, manifest the repressed drives of that unconscious. Further, illusion, which is grounded in imagination, is the only feature of our work-oriented civilization that is *play-oriented*; it is only the imagination to which *free play* is allowed. Genet, who perhaps goes further in his use of illusion than most artists, falls into a special category that Freud also describes—the artist who tries to re-create the world in his own imagination, erasing distasteful features and replacing them with others more in conformity with his desires.

The reader apprehends in Genet just such an attempt as described by Freud to *re-create* the world as he (Genet) desires it to be. In this connection, the analogy between the words "play" and "recreation" becomes important. As Erik Erikson indicates in his study *Childhood and Society* (New York, 1963, pp.212–213), when a man plays, he is outside the sphere of social and economic reality. In other words, he does not work. He escapes into a world with specific space and time limitations where he does not have to consider "reality" (e.g., a chess match, played on a small board during a previously agreed-upon span of time). Play, for the most part, becomes a pleasurable but temporary escape from the work-a-day world. It is a periodic journey into the timeless world of the "interior man" in quest of a kind of renovation of the psyche. To the adult who spends most of his time working, play is, more than ever, *re-creation*. It allows him to escape from time to time from the limitations of his social reality, which tend to sap his psychic vitality. Play, then, may be, quite literally, *a re-creation of the world in one's imagination so that the newly re-created world may become a source of pleasure;* that is, play may be the creation of an illusion. In this, as has been shown, it is at one with art and the enjoyment of art. And in its wish-fulfillment aspect, it is at one with the realm of dreams, which are a manifestation of the unconscious.

For Genet, play encompasses a number of areas, all of which occur repeatedly in his works. Among these correlatives of play are impersonation, play-acting, illusion, dream, ritual, myth, and negation. It seems self-evident that impersonation and play-acting (i.e., playing at being someone else) are correlatives of play, and that illusion and dream exist also within the realm of play. But what of ritual, myth, and negation? How are they related to play? If we look at ritual for a moment, it becomes relatively easy to see its origins in play and illusion. Ritual centers on the mystical achievement of many desires; through it, man rises above the monotony of everyday living, and he transcends the real world. It is, however, more than a sham reality, for it is an "actualization by representation." The participants in a ritual are convinced that their symbolic actions effect a definite higher state of being, a reordering of the world—at least temporarily—

on the level of unattainable desires; in short, it is wish-fulfillment. At the same time, the rite retains other characteristics of play. For instance, it is performed within a limited space that is a temporary real world of its own. And its communicants share in the "make-believe" world with the utmost seriousness. [2]

Myth, like ritual, represents an attempt to overcome the limitations and obstacles of the world of reality. Archetypal mythic figures symbolize and "actualize" man's deepest longings. Oedipus at Colonus, for example, represents mankind's triumph over sorrow, shame, and death. The eternal cyclical return of Dionysus also signifies triumph over death. In the realm of myth, all the laws of "reality" are suspended or negated—and negation, too, is an aspect of play for Genet.

The nature of Genet's play invariably involves negation; it is satanic and evil, not the kind usually thought of as childlike and innocent. What then is the connection between Genet's play-activity (i.e., his art) and his satanism and negation? If we remember that negation usually involves some sort of liberation, we can begin to comprehend its relationship to play. The connection between the two, for Genet, is the attempt to assert what Herbert Marcuse calls the "order of sensuousness" over the "order of reason," for civilization has caused reason to dominate sensuousness to an overwhelming extent. Reason, Marcuse says, impoverishes and barbarizes sensuousness, and he defines the play impulse as liberation from reality:

> The impulse does not aim at playing "with" something; rather it is the play of life itself, beyond want and external compulsion— the manifestation of freedom itself. Man is free only when . . . he is constrained neither by law nor by need, but such constraint *is* the reality. Freedom is thus . . . freedom from the established reality. [3]

How can we correlate what we know of Genet's play impulse with Marcuse's definition of that impulse? Certainly, Genet's play impulse manifests freedom, but, with his freedom, Genet engages in the play of evil. Is it only because the play impulse in Genet becomes a negative force to assert itself more forcefully? Perhaps, but it would seem, at the same time, that the play impulse, even in Genet, is positive in that it *liberates*. What it liberates in him is *his negation of the "straight" world*. Genet, the pariah-criminal, re-creates himself in the world of his own devising—art—which parodies the satanism of life. And Genet's works ordinarily portray him as a child-seer whose genius is in inventing play-forms suited to his assumed role and self-appointed tasks. He destroys the existing good "real" world, therefore, only in order to re-create it through his art in the play of his imagination; that is, through the use of illusion.

Genet engages in playing the game of illusion with all the profound seriousness that children evince when they play certain of their games. The allusion to children's games is apt because, though serious, Genet's works strike one as playful in both conception and execution. Although the concepts of seriousness and play may seem, at first glance, to be mutually inimical, in fact the two categories converge. One has only to envision a bridge tournament or a football game to realize how play and seriousness may often coincide. And what can be more serious than a child's game of "house" or "cops and robbers"?

Mere mimesis, then, is not the function of Genet's art; it is, rather, the *play of illusion* and *illusion as play* that become the major themes of his works. His characters—indeed, even he himself—become immersed in illusion because illusion (and dream, for that matter) is the wish-fulfillment expression of the unconscious. In this, as has been shown, it occupies a common ground with dream and play. Because they succeed in expressing the feared unconscious, which is otherwise repressed by civilization's reality principle, illusion and play probably express a deeper reality than "reality." In fact, as Johan Huizinga states in his brilliant essay on the play element in society, *Homo Ludens* (Boston, 1950), the very word *illusion* becomes pregnant with meaning when we realize its Latin root is *in-ludere*, which means, quite literally, "in-play." He says also that in the participant's complete absorption in the illusionary aspect of play lies the essence, the primeval quality, of play. Moreover, the "fun" of playing depends upon the degree of the participant's absorption in illusion—and fun, like play, can be a "serious" matter. There is no doubt that it is so for Genet.

Play, then, becomes in Genet's eyes a complex vehicle for

his ideas—a vehicle in which, like his own favorite symbol, the mirror, the images of play proliferate almost endlessly to embrace areas sometimes not ordinarily associated with it. For him, play is equated with illusion, dream, play-acting, impersonation, ritual, myth, and negation—all attributes that liberate the shackled unconscious from the repressions of the real world. And he profanizes play to the extent that it becomes *evil*, for evil is a negation too, a negation of the good, pure, bourgeois, "real" world, which Genet taunts with his visions.

Inevitably, Genet eventually projected his taunting, nightmarish visions on the screen best designed to reflect them—the drama. He became especially interested in the theatre, it seems, after discovering the dramatic theories of Antonin Artaud. Artaud's Theatre of Cruelty was almost made to order for Genet, and he immediately began to incorporate elements from it into his plays, starting with his third drama, *The Balcony*, and adding more elements with each succeeding theatrical work he produced until, with the last drama he wrote, *The Screens*, he might be said to have attained a true Theatre of Cruelty. No one seems certain when Genet first discovered Artaud's theories, but to attempt to discover exactly when he came upon Artaud's work seems pointless as well as fruitless. The fact is that he *did* discover Artaud around 1954, since he praised the work of the dramatic theorist in a letter written in that year to J. J. Pauvert. And he seems to have embraced Artraud's theories. As Robert Brustein points out, Genet may be said to be Artaud's Sophocles.

Once the principles of the Theatre of Cruelty have been stated, it is easy to comprehend why they should have captured Genet's imagination. First, Artaud places primary stress on the importance of *spectacle* in the theatre. The *mise-en-scène*, he declares, is paramount and not to be subordinated to the written word. Lighting, costume, gesture, and mime are all as important as the words in the wholly integrated drama. Artaud cites Oriental, particularly Balinese, theatre as an example of the perfect *mise-en-scène*, for it incorporates lighting, gesture, costume, mime, and language into a unified whole.

Moreover, language, when used in Western theatre, he says, should be used as incantation as in Oriental theatre. He indicates

Western theatre's worship of the Word as odious; the theatre in the West is merely a branch of literature. He would not do away with speech entirely; rather, he would change its role to one of submission to the spectacle. He would employ it only to enhance the scope of the drama.

In many ways, Artaud's theories presage Marshall McLuhan's concept of literate Western Man's "linearity." Since print—as in a dramatic text—must be linear and since literate man must learn to read in a linear fashion, he too becomes "linear" (i.e., oriented toward the idea of continuum, or sequentiality, of thought or feeling; "fragmented," or compartmentalized, in his thinking) as opposed to the integrated tribal man, who, for instance, does not separate art from life nor the individual from the group. Literate Western Man's linearity is recapitulated also in his linear concept of time. As Mircea Eliade indicates in *Myth and Reality*, Western Christianity is almost alone among world religions in its insistence upon the "linear Time of History: the World was created once and will have only one end; the Incarnation took place only once, in historical Time, and there will be only one Judgment."[4] Conversely, the non-Christian, nonliterate man views time as cyclical and integral. To the pre-Christian, preliterate German, for instance, *Götterdämmerung* was merely the prelude to the time when the earth would be born anew. Moreover, the ancient Greek god Dionysus died and was resurrected periodically. And, of course, I have already spoken elsewhere of the integral Taoist symbol.

An integral theatre, then, is possible only in the context of an integral society, and Artaud finds that integrated theatre in Bali, where the theatre draws "upon dance, song, pantomime—and a little of the theater as we understand it in the Occident—[and] restores the theater, by means of ceremonies of indubitable age and well-tried efficacy, to its original destiny, which it presents as a combination of all these elements fused together in a perspective of hallucination and fear."[5] The performances of Balinese theatre, in other words, constitute *rituals*, and ritual, for Artaud as for Genet, is as important as the spectacle. Theatre should not merely "entertain" for an evening, should not amuse uselessly with a cheap imitation of "reality." It should, instead, express the soul's reality. It should, like Oriental theatre, have a metaphysical quality and not, like Occidental theatre, a psychological one. The audience, too, becomes important in the Theatre of Cruelty. Ideally, the spectacle should surround the audience so that it becomes engulfed in what happens. The theatre should furnish spectators with a view of their own internal world—their erotic desires, their repressed longings, their savagery—expose them to a reality that is far more "real" than external reality. The spectacle should drench the audience in a violence that will duplicate the violence of its own thoughts. Artaud defies "any spectator to whom such violent scenes will have transferred their blood . . . to give himself up, once outside the theatre, to ideas of war, riot, and blatant murder."[6]

In other words, a kind of Aristotelian purgation of cruelty should occur. Consequently, the audience *must*, as in a serious game or ritual, identify strongly with the spectacle. In order for this identification to occur, the theatre should choose themes consistent with the agitation and neurosis of the twentieth century; these themes should be cosmic in scope. They should, at all costs, reflect man's unfulfilled longings, his repressed desires, his fearsome, terror-inspiring, unknown innermost Self—which, paradoxically, is not Self at all, but that *Other*, Other only because civilized man has denied conscious expression to it.

It should now be easy to understand why Genet was irresistibly drawn to Artaudian dramatic theories: they incorporate almost entirely his visionary concept of profane play as the reflection of contemporary man's soul.

1 | THE EARLY WORKS*

The Beginnings

To mention Jean Genet's name to those acquainted with his drama is to conjure up visions of criminality, evil, perversion, betrayal, and abjection. And there can be no doubt that all of these elements exist in his work, for he is devoted to a world that is a photographic negative of the world as perceived by most of his intellectual peers. Genet's is a world in which all of the traditionally accepted values are rejected and in which moral concepts traditionally spurned as objectionable are sanctified and enshrined.

That the land which produced Villon, de Sade, Baudelaire, and Rimbaud should also produce a Genet is not so unusual. What *is* perhaps unusual is the adulation accorded to him in France today. Part of this fame stems, no doubt, from the aura of *succès de scandale* that has emanated from his works. Nevertheless, the almost universal critical acclaim which his works have encountered indicates that their content expresses some unnameable—but finally recognized—trait in man that is attracted by evil, by death, and by perversion.

But how can a dramatist, having arrived at such a "negative" morality, brandish it like some black-flamed torch at midday in front of his audience? By what means does a man come to worship evil and to write of his revelation in much the same way

---

*A condensation of this chapter appeared as "Jean Genet as *Homo Ludens* in Quest of Profane Play," *Connecticut Review*, Vol. VI, No. 1 (© 1972 by the Board of Trustees for the Connecticut State Colleges), pp. 26-33.

that others have written of the revelation of God? Other than finding answers to these questions in the works of the author himself or in his infrequent autobiographical pronouncements, the interested reader must turn to the monumental study of Genet by Jean-Paul Sartre, *Saint Genet, Actor and Martyr* (*Saint Genet, comédien et martyr*). According to some commentators, it is rather unfortunate to have to study Sartre. It is undoubtedly true, for instance, that, although he frequently has brilliant and ingenious critical insights into Genet's character and his works, Sartre not infrequently polemicizes, attempting to depict Genet as a prototype of the Existentialist hero or to proselytize in the Marxist cause. Nevertheless, Sartre does appear to be the one person who truly knows most of the facts of Genet's life, and there can be little doubt that his analysis of his subject's childhood is valid in view of subsequent events in Genet's life.

Sartre divides Genet's life into two unequal parts, which might be entitled "Before the Fall" and "After the Fall." The "Satan" of this contemporary *Paradise Lost* is created as follows:

> A child dies of shame, and a hoodlum takes his place; the hoodlum will be haunted by the child. We should really speak of resurrection, evoke the ancient initiation rituals of shamanism and of secret societies except that Genet categorically refuses to be "reborn." He has died; that is all. And Genet is nothing more than a dead man. [1]

In a sense, Genet passes from one "nonstate" to another. As an illegitimate child placed under the guardianship of some peasants, the young Jean has no status. To be legitimate means to be "owned" by a family and, in turn, to "own" that family. It means, as Sartre indicates, to be the eventual possessor of the family's land and goods. To be an abandoned bastard like Genet means to be disowned, no more than a bit of excrement eliminated from his mother's system. It means, above all, never to inherit land and goods—an unnatural state in a society where possession is the keystone of legitimacy, of acceptance. What, then, could be less astonishing than for the young Genet to endeavor to acquire possessions? Sartre relates how the child begins to secure possessions through a favorite game, thievery. But the thefts, Sartre maintains, are performed in complete innocence, for they are acts executed by the boy's loathesome body, a repugnant object "defecated" from an unknown womb and forsaken as so much waste; they are not acts performed by the disembodied spirit, which tends to retain its "saintliness" because it is not implicated in what the repellent body does. Nevertheless, the baubles that result from Genet's play-activity do gratify his spiritual craving for status in the society in which he is being reared. As Sartre indicates, to own a thing is to *use* it without having to say, "Merci, monsieur." And so the trinkets which the boy has filched, he can use as much as he desires when he is alone. He has attained a certain amount of "status" through his game. The pleasure derived from fruits of his "sinful" activity thus perplexes the child, a perplexity that is the beginning of his conversion to the cause of evil.

But, at the age of ten Genet is caught, and the accusations that assail him he finds appalling. He is an ingrate, a thief, a monster, his "goodness" merely a deception enabling him the better to practice his thefts. Now a complete transformation occurs. If his "goodness" is a deception and, in reality, an evil, then so be it—let all goodness be evil. And if his pleasurable game of thievery is evil, then let all evil be good. As in some primitive rite in which, by calling an object by a name, that object metamorphoses into the thing named, so Genet, because he is named "thief," becomes a thief. And he is cast out of his childhood paradise; he will, like Satan, mock that paradise henceforth.

There is one redeeming feature in his condemnation: the child intuits that he has only been "lent" to these peasants. And, though earlier in his life he may have regretted that he didn't "belong" to them, it is now the very fact of his not belonging that makes their condemnation bearable. Sartre tells us that Genet senses his difference from those around him from the beginning; he is the bastard and the outcast. His difference is confirmed all too terribly when his thefts are discovered. If he is a thief—and he undoubtedly is—then it follows that he is an object of loathing, just like the excrement he feels himself to be. He is that in human nature which is despised, that which is dark and evil, that which is suppressed. In short, he is the *Other*, and he now makes a conscious effort to assert that Other in himself, indeed, to celebrate it. He rejects the good, bourgeois, "white" world in favor of the evil, criminal, "black" world. Consequently, at the age of fifteen, he is incarcerated in the reformatory at Mettray as a recalcitrant thief. In a sense, it is a homecoming for Genet, who is, after all, the child of government institutions. He began his life as a ward of the state, and now he is again a ward of the state. So much the better if his spiritual "mother" harbors criminals, for he now belongs in their milieu. But, by what Sartre calls *"le miracle d'horreur,"* even the society of criminals, the brotherhood of evil, rejects him. To them, he is a soft, effeminate bourgeois, a "fairy." Once again, abjection and humiliation become Genet's lot—a lot which he learns to accept even to the point of actively becoming the "fairy" he has been called. If he is to be the Eternal Outcast, the complete Other, then abjection will be his pride. And, since he is to be completely alone in the universe, in order to complete his abjection and to deserve it, he will assume, in time, the badge of the absolute pariah, betrayal— the sin that revolts both the criminal and the noncriminal societies.

Through all his subsequent sojourns as thief, homosexual, traitor, prostitute, and jailbird, Genet retains a sort of negative state of grace. All of his life becomes a fascinating game of "loser wins," in which "Lower is higher, perseverance in evil is the way to saintliness, betrayal is devotion, and the mask is more nearly real than what it covers."[2] Genet's game often sustains him when all else in his life miscarries. Thus, in fantasy, he may revel in the damnation which society has visited upon him, for those "who are damned by society are, according to Genet, also damned by God. But in that very fact is to be seen their . . . glory. Genet sees it as a limitation of God that He cannot experience damnation."[3] Damnation means the revelation of the Void, of Evil, from all of which the good bourgeois recoils in horror. It is a necessary corollary of Genet's game that the loser force the winner to descry that terrible Other, for therein lies part of the loser's victory.

In an important way, Genet's homosexuality apotheosizes his "loser wins" philosophy. Invariably, Genet is the submissive partner in the homosexual affair, the better to be humiliated. It is he who is entered by his lover in the act of sodomy; it is he who fellates his love-partner. Yet, in a paradoxical way, by debasing himself, Genet the "fairy" somehow triumphs over his lordly, contemptuous pimp, for the pimp is, after all, quite dependent upon the "fairy" for his sexual pleasure. To attain his orgasm, the pimp must allow himself to be "engulfed" by the contemptible "fairy."

In this triumph of submission over dominance, Genet perceives another element that enhances the attraction the homosexual love rite holds for him, and that element is the most sanctified (for Genet) of unholy acts, betrayal. It does not escape Genet's attention that, while the phallus of the pimp becomes detumescent upon the attainment of orgasm, his own remains rigid and erect. The "fairy" is "alive"; the pimp, "dead," figuratively murdered by the "fairy." Moreover, in such an act as anal intercourse, the pimp literally plunges his erect, vital phallus into excrement. In fellatio, on the other hand, he allows his erect member to melt, in the words of Sartre, like sugar on the tongue. Homosexuality, consequently, amounts to a betrayal of the pimp's manhood. On a more universal level, any act of homosexuality symbolizes to Genet the archetypal traitor, for the homosexual is thrice-traitor—traitor to nature, traitor to his sex, and traitor to his lover.

What had previously been merely symbolic victories in the game of "loser wins," glimpsed only in fantasy, suddenly transformed themselves into an actual victory in the year 1947. In that year, Genet, the alarming recidivist who had been sentenced to life imprisonment some time before on his tenth conviction for theft, found himself a *cause célèbre*. The intellectual community of France clamored for his release from prison on the grounds that he was an important artist, and it sent a petition to the president of the Republic, who duly pardoned Genet, subsequently summoning him to dinner in the presidential palace. And so the pariah and the president broke bread together. How ironic it must have seemed to Jean Genet—bastard, thief, prostitute, "fairy," convict, traitor, and now *artist!*

There are critics who feel that Sartre's monumental study constitutes an obstacle to a completely objective study of Genet because, having read Sartre's book, the reader experiences great difficulty in viewing Genet from any point of view other than Sartre's. The work is, nevertheless, still extremely important in understanding Genet's thievery, his "saintly" criminality, his satanism, and his *oeuvre*. In the final analysis, one is inclined to the judgment that, despite his undisputed biases, Sartre undoubtedly knows and understands Genet, perhaps better than any other living person. We have Genet's own word on that score. Moreover, when an important writer and philosopher with the artistic integrity of Jean-Paul Sartre takes upon himself the task of writing a monumental study of a relatively obscure pornographer, it is obviously *not* with the primary intent of expounding his own political or social philosophy. We must conclude that he sees in his subject an important artistic talent—so important that he feels him worthy of a profoundly searching six hundred page biocritical analysis. Without Sartre's study, as a matter of fact, there is good reason to doubt whether Genet, though a worthy artist, would ever have been placed so high in the artistic firmament so soon—a position in that firmament which few critics would dispute today.

Joseph McMahon, however, in his critical work *The Imagination of Jean Genet* takes issue with Sartre over the causes of Genet's homosexuality and criminality. He maintains that Sartre is inept in his handling of Genet's criminality and sexual deviation because the French philosopher finds great complexity in Genet's rather simple quest for sexual enjoyment with other men. McMahon contends that it is not an unwholesome, "rotten" bourgeois society that is at fault for Genet's homosexuality but rather Genet's own simple sexual responses to a set of given erotic situations at a specific moment in time. The bourgeoisie, he says, cannot be blamed for those specific moments that become the occasions for Genet's deviant activities. But McMahon seems to do an injustice to Sartre. Sartre does not blame Genet's "specific moments" of homosexual activity on the bourgeoisie any more than he blames this class for any one specific crime Genet may have committed. Rather, he dispassionately charges it with the *occasions* that caused—and, indeed, forced—Genet to assume the role of Other; that is, to assume the mantle of Evil, symbolized by traits that the bourgeois society hated and feared:

thievery, homosexuality, and treachery, among others. But buggery, betrayal, and theft are merely manifestations of Evil and are subsidiary to it. Consequently, Sartre does not point an accusing finger at society every time Genet picks up a pretty young man or filches a handsome silver platter; to do so would be petty, not to mention banal, and a bit stupid. What interests Sartre is the fact that, like an Existentialist hero, Genet *accepts* his role as the opponent of the good, the decent, the bourgeois. Like Camus's Sisyphus, Genet learns to accept, even to enjoy, the role in which a hated society has cast him. It is in his acceptance of the role allotted him that Genet triumphs.

In an interview published in *Playboy* in April of 1964, Genet said, in answer to a question put to him about his homosexuality, thievery, and betrayal:

> I made no decision. If I began to steal, it was because I was hungry. Then I had to justify my act, I had to accept it. As for being homosexual, I can't tell you why I am. I know nothing about it. Does anyone know why one is homosexual? . . . Homosexuality was . . . thrust upon me, like the color of my eyes, the number of my feet. As a child, I was aware that I was attracted by boys. It's only after experiencing that attraction that I "decided" that I freely *chose* my homosexuality, in the Sartrian sense of the word "choose." To put it more simply: I had to put up with it, to come to terms with it, *even though I knew it was damned by society.* [4] [Italics mine]

It might almost be a speech spoken by the hero of a contemporary Existentialist novel or drama. No recriminations against society, just an acceptance of the facts of one's existence to the point where that acceptance becomes a choice in spite of the consequences.

In the same *Playboy* interview, Genet says of Sartre's *Saint Genet:*

> I saw myself stripped naked—by someone other than myself. I strip myself in all my books, but at the same time I disguise myself with words, with attitudes . . . by means of a certain magic. I manage not to get too damaged. But I was stripped by Sartre unceremoniously. My first impulse was to burn the book. . . . I let him publish it because my chief concern has

always been to be responsible for my acts. It took me some time to get over my reading of his book. I was almost unable to continue writing. . . .

. . . .

I remained in that awful state for six years.[5]

If Sartre's work so shook Genet that he was unable to write for a number of years, then it is certainly safe to assume that Sartre, in good part, hit the mark in his analysis of Genet.

It is probably true that Genet chose evil, in part, to create a necessary tension between good and evil, with both moral qualities mutually dependent upon the other as its *raison d'être*. It is certainly true that this tension is part of Genet's aesthetic. Genet makes a coherent system of evil in order to pose it against good. If we bear in mind the Taoist symbol that introduced this book, it becomes easier now to relate it to Genet.

Genet, then, chose as his own the world of those values that were opposed to the good bourgeois values; that is, the world of the mirror image, of the photographic negative, of nihilism, of stasis, of betrayal, and of death. And Sartre analyzed the reasons behind this choice perhaps better than any other commentator. It now remains to investigate how Genet's philosophical and aesthetic vision developed and deepened as his literary career progressed.

The Nondramatic Prose Works

While in prison from 1942 on, Genet began to write a series of books that established his underground reputation as an artist and led to his subsequent pardon. These works are interesting for a number of reasons, not the least of which is their unashamed pornography. They express, sometimes in lyrical language, a ritual adoration of betrayal, perversion, and crime, especially theft and murder. Illustrating his developing ideas about death, criminality, betrayal—the saintliness of evil—these books exemplify, above all, Genet's growing preoccupation with the correlation between these "saintly" traits and the concept of profane play.

Genet's first major prose work, *Our Lady of the Flowers* (*Notre-Dame-des-Fleurs*), grew out of the author's desire to create an occasion for "playing with himself." The book begins, beyond any doubt, as a masturbatory fantasy—indeed, Sartre has called it the epic of masturbation. Genet, incarcerated in the prison at Fresnes, calls up various images to help him achieve orgasm. The images become transformed into characters and the tale, such as it is, begins. Divine, an aging homosexual "queen," begins to lose his lovers to a young, handsome homosexual, Our Lady of the Flowers, who has arrived on the Parisian scene. In the course of the tale, we discover that Our Lady, before his encounter with Divine, has gratuitously killed an old man. Divine's emotional composure and his physical constitution disintegrate slowly as he watches Our Lady's ascendancy. But Our Lady is apprehended in a dope raid and, during the course of a police interrogation, confesses to the murder of the old man in the same gratuitous fashion in which he committed the crime in the first place. He is convicted of the crime at about the same time that Divine expires of tuberculosis. Thus, the story ends.

It is rather difficult even to relate the simple story line sketched above because one wishes always to refer to Divine in the feminine. Genet is more than successful in convincing us that Divine's masculinity has been totally subjugated by his desire to be a female, that Divine is so thoroughly immersed in his game of illusion, his masquerade as a woman, that he is more truly "she" than "he," even though "realistically" he is a male. The reason Genet convinces us of Divine's feminine essence cannot be casually attributed to artistic dexterity, for the plot is not truly important. Whatever sense we find in the novel must come from our comprehension of the author's developing notions of play.

His next book, *Miracle of the Rose* (*Miracle de la Rose*), is also steeped in his sense of homosexuality as illusion. It is set in the prison of Fontevrault and is supposedly an autobiographical account of Genet's stay there. The story is interwoven, however, with reminiscences of the author's boyhood experiences at the Mettray Reformatory, presented in such a manner that both levels of time, the past and the present, seem to operate concurrently. The occasion for the book is a paean to an Unholy Trinity: Harcamone, a condemned murderer; Bulkaen, a young, handsome tough; and Divers, an old acquaintance of Genet's from Mettray. All three have been sentenced to the Fontevrault Prison and are already there when Genet arrives:

> Through Harcamone, Divers, and Bulkaen, I shall relive
> again the Mettray days that were my childhood. I shall find
> again the abolished penal colony, the destroyed children's
> reformatory.[6]

Genet, by "cannibalizing" and absorbing their spiritual sub-
stance in homosexually inspired remembrances and visions of
them, symbolically unites all three in his own being and in so
doing attains the Godhead of Evil—which is to say, he attains the
illusion of Godhead, its mirror image. He presides as chief celeb-
rant, God-King, at the solemn rites in his world of illusion. Time
has no relevance in this world where the author juxtaposes scenes
from childhood with those from adulthood to spin out his ritual
obeisance to Death and illusion. The death of Harcamone, the
death of Bulkaen, the death of his childhood—all are the same to
Genet; that is, the attainment of a sort of negative apotheosis:

> Harcamone is dead, Bulkaen is dead. If I leave [this prison],
> I am going to search through the old newspapers as I did after
> the death of Pilorge. As it was with Pilorge, there won't be
> anything in my hands but a very brief news account on poor
> paper, a sort of gray ash that will show me that he was executed
> at dawn. These newspapers are their tomb. *But I shall transmit
> their names far into time. These names, alone, will remain in the
> future, relieved of their bodies.* We may ask, who were Bulkaen,
> Harcamone, Divers; who was Pilorge; who was Guy? *And their
> names will disturb us as the light that comes from a star dead a thousand
> years disturbs us.* Have I said everything I had to say about this
> adventure? *If I leave this book, I leave what can be recounted. The
> rest is indescribable. I keep quiet and walk barefoot.*[7] [Italics mine]

It matters not one whit that the names of Harcamone, Bulkaen,
and Divers will attain immortality by having their stories inscribed in Genet's book, for, like the star whose light reaches the
earth a thousand years after the star itself has died, they will long
since have ceased to exist; they will have long since attained the
state of nonbeing, of stasis, of timelessness, which, paradoxically,
is at the core of being. It is just *that* very fact which cannot be
recounted, which is mystical and ineffable, and before which
Genet becomes silent and removes his shoes in humility.

The next work by Genet was *Funeral Rites* (*Pompes funèbres*). He says, in the first few paragraphs of the book, "la mort de Jean D. . . . donne prétexte à ce livre." It would not be amiss to say that the book is a protracted ritual, an obsequy in honor of Jean, in honor of death, in honor of betrayal. I shall describe later how Genet makes rituals of most of his dramas also. *Funeral Rites* opens with the liberation of Paris in August of 1945. During the last days of the Resistance, Genet's friend and sometime lover, Jean, has been shot by the Gestapo as a member of the Underground. Genet and Jean's fiancée have returned from the morgue where they have identified Jean's body. Arrangements are made for Jean's funeral. Jean's mother, his fiancée, and his friend Genet will attend the services. Shortly thereafter, Genet goes to a movie where he views a newsreel of the fighting between the Germans and the Maquis, and a curious sensation comes over him: he finds himself sympathizing with an SS trooper and a young French collaborator against the French forces. The SS man in the film reminds him of Erik, Jean's mother's lover (who, it is intimated, has had something to do with Jean's death), and Genet now finds that he loves Erik. The film triggers a tale within the tale already begun, yet running parallel with it, a tale involving Erik and his homosexual lover, Riton (an imaginary character based on the young French collaborator in the film). The two threads, one imaginary, the other "actual," intertwine and become entangled with philosophical observations. Funeral preparations continue, Erik and Riton undergo all their adventures, and Genet's asides become interspersed with both.

Among the most important features of the novel is Genet's transference of love from the dead Jean to the living Erik (or is it the imaginary Erik?). Tantamount to a betrayal of Jean, this transference of love, nonetheless, is consistent with Genet's philosophy. Erik, who has, in some way, been responsible for Jean's death, must obviously be superior to Jean. To love Erik, then, is to love a higher embodiment of the beauty that was Jean. Erik, the representation of Evil, has bested Jean, the symbol of Good. Erik is handsome as Jean had been handsome. But Erik becomes the reverse of the coin, as it were: Erik is criminal;

Jean was heroic. The most important feature of Erik's attraction for Genet is moral rather than physical, for Erik performs his evil deeds *wilfully*. Furthermore, Erik, as a representative of an army and a nation on their way to imminent defeat exudes an aura of humiliation that could only heighten his attraction to Genet. Evil, abjection, murder—it is no great wonder that Genet betrays the memory of Jean for Erik, for the SS man has attained "sainthood" in Genet's eyes and is, therefore, worthy of adoration.

Querelle of Brest (*Querelle de Brest*), Genet's next novel, centers on a handsome sailor, Querelle, who is also a murderer. Querelle exclaims at one point in the book, "I'm not a fairy, you know. I like girls." Nevertheless, he frequently engages in homosexual acts.

Querelle has arrived in town, and, with the rest of the crew of the ship, he is on leave. His superior officer, Lieutenant Seblon, is in love with Querelle, but he confides his longings only to his journal, from which entries recur again and again during the narrative. Soon after his arrival, Querelle commits a murder and frames someone else for the crime. It is not Querelle's first murder; in the past, he has killed Joachim, a homosexual with whom he was involved. Because homosexuality and murder have some connection within Querelle's mind, the sailor feels compelled, after his second murder, to subject himself to a sodomistic union with Nono, husband to Madame Lysiane, the local brothel keeper. Later in the novel, Querelle, after arousing Mario, the chief of police, fellates him. He becomes involved with a number of people, including Mme. Lysiane, his brother Robert, and a young man whose name is Gil. After betraying Gil to the police, Querelle leaves Brest, having profoundly affected the lives of those with whom he had become associated.

In one important scene, Querelle refuses to consummate an act of love to the point of orgasm with Gil. The significance of the scene lies in Querelle's refusal to be "betrayed," for it is quite clear that he is the "male" in his relationship with Gil—and it is the "male" who is betrayed in the homosexual act. Moreover, Querelle has already literally betrayed Gil to the police. He must play the game of Judas to the end, having already murdered at least two people and "betrayed" (i.e., played the "female" to) two others, Nono and Mario.

Thief's Journal (Journal du voleur), Genet's last major prose work, is a quasi-autobiographical account of his adventures throughout Europe in the pre-World War II period. He recounts these escapades as his imagination has retained them, ill-defined, blurred, with some events remembered more vividly or more accurately than others. Time has added or subtracted details from recollections of characters or events. In other words, Genet has again immersed himself in the playful world of imagination and illusion. One of the threads that weaves itself through the book as a unifying force is the childlike quality of the hoodlums and "queers"; in fact, the whole existence of these characters hinges in great part upon their childlike ability to engage in what amounts to a long, but perverted, game:

> Stilitano was no more a mature man than I myself was. . . . *he played at being a gangster; that is to say that he used to invent postures. I don't know any hoodlums who aren't children.* [Italics mine] What "serious" soul, if he passes in front of a jewelry shop or a bank makes up carefully and gravely the details of an attack or a burglary? . . . He tried to imitate an ideal hero, the Stilitano whose image was already inscribed in a glorious heaven.[8]

Games, masquerade, illusion—all these aspects of play are at the heart of Genet's nondramatic prose works. In scene after scene from the books, we have witnessed betrayal as a game, crime as play, and impersonation as an expression of role-playing. In *Our Lady of the Flowers*, for instance, we are confronted with scenes of masquerade and impersonation, most of which revolve around homosexuals in "drag." The "queens" plunge themselves into the illusion of a feminine nature, even though their femininity is quite obviously belied by masculine sexual accoutrements. The illusionism of the "queens" becomes especially heightened during the weekly Thursday night "drag" balls held at Le Tavernacle, one of which is described in detail by Genet. There is an almost cinematic quality about this description, with its "dissolves" and montage sequences; it conveys the sense of illusion as in a dream or a film. The same cinematic quality attaches to *Funeral Rites*, in which the "imaginary" action within the "actual" story is actually triggered by a film which Genet views. *Miracle of the Rose*, too, displays the illusionary cinematic technique of Genet in its frequent flashbacks to Mettray.

When it comes to a discussion of meanings in these works, I must admonish the reader that the Frenchman's works are not prone to tidy discussion concerning illusion and reality. No sooner has the reader felt that he has apprehended the meaning of a work than he finds something in the work that seems to contradict that apprehension. Bearing this warning in mind, the reader may, nonetheless, assume that Genet attempts to indicate something about his characters' imprisonment in illusion. Perhaps the easiest illustration of a character's imprisonment in illusion to be found in any of Genet's books is in *Thief's Journal*. Stilitano, one of Genet's beloved "mec"s, is quite literally imprisoned in a hall of mirrors in an amusement park in Antwerp. His imprisonment symbolizes his illusions concerning his own virility and his power—illusions that entrap him, for his virility and his power are symbolically sapped from him by his pretty young male lover (or, for that matter, by any homosexual lover when we remember that such is the nature of the inverted love affair that the "dominant" male must submit to the "submissive" male to achieve orgasm). Significantly, Stilitano must be extricated from his "prison" by his young male lover.

In like fashion, the other works display characters trapped in a mirror world. Mirrors assume an important role in almost all of Genet's major works; they, of course, represent illusion. And illusion is nonbeing—the static, unchanging state around which *being* (or reality) revolves, much like the unmoving point at the hub of a turning wheel. It is not a topsy-turvy world, therefore, in which nonbeing becomes reality and being becomes illusion. What man is pleased to call "illusion" is, in truth, the most expressive reality, for illusion is just a "front" for nonbeing. *But* escape into nonbeing is impossible because nonbeing is unknowable. Consequently, such characters as the masqueraders in *Our Lady of the Flowers* are deluded when they feel they have escaped into illusion, for, in every case, the fantasies of the impersonators reflect desires to attain states of *being* which they would like to achieve in the "real" world; i.e., the "drag queens" dress like women. Illusion, paradoxically, is that which does not exist, and, therefore, the fantasy into which the impersonators feel they escape is really imprisonment in an "illusion of illusion."

Genet himself, in a sense, is imprisoned in his own imagination, for he is at the center of all his works. *Thief's Journal* and *Miracle of the Rose* constitute his memoirs; the other works represent his own fantasies. He is, for instance, to a great extent the character Divine in *Our Lady of the Flowers*. At the same time, he is a sort of unseen observer of the action, for the book is his own dream, a masturbatory fantasy called up from the realm of illusion. He is the unmoving center around which the action of the novel revolves. In the final analysis, Genet illustrates his own imprisonment in illusion just as surely as he has shown his characters'.

We must remember, however, that, for Genet, imprisonment does not hold the same terror as it might hold for the ordinary man. After all, as Sartre points out, prison is Genet's symbolic mother. He became a ward of the state when he was an infant farmed out to foster parents. Later, when he was imprisoned at Mettray, Fresnes, Fontevrault, and other prisons, he grew to feel a kinship with the governmental punitive institutions. Consequently, in Genet's view, imprisonment in illusion is ultimately man's only hope. In a world where the loser invariably wins and where abjection is invariably exaltation, imprisonment must be equated with freedom. And by submitting to the world of illusion, man attains true mastery over the world of reality.

2 | THE FIRST DRAMAS

In view of Genet's fast-developing interest in the world of play and illusion, it is not surprising that he finally turned to the theatre as his primary artistic instrument. In the novels, he could recreate the world of his imagination only to a limited extent, for words kept getting in the way, inhibiting the scope of his vision, restricting his vision within words on a printed page. And this limitation inhibited his power to convey his world of fantasy to the imagination of the reader. And a reader, by the very nature of the act of reading, is not *involved* to any significant degree in what he reads, for, as Marshall McLuhan says in *The Gutenberg Galaxy* (Toronto, 1962), the "interiorization of the technology of the phonetic alphabet translates man from the magical world of the ear to the neutral visual world." The world of the theatre, however, restores the primacy of the magical and tribal aural world, in which viewers both listen to and watch the ritual spectacle intently to become immersed in it, for the spectacle should set up mystical "vibrations" within the participants. Moreover, the theatre employs its aural approach to art within the context of fantasy and play. The theatre is illusion insofar as it is not "real life"; the actors and the audience, after all, leave the theatre to enter the real world after the performance is over. Simultaneously, the theatre is play because actors "play" at being other people in a drama created out of the "play" of the author's imagination. The attraction of the theatre for Genet was, therefore, almost inevitable.

Nevertheless, nothing could have attracted Genet less than the bourgeois *théâtre du boulevard* with its straightforward stories and its neat little morals, with its "true-to-life" characters and realistic settings, with its psychological probings into motivation and its attempts to pose answers to problems. Nor could certain aspects of the much more experimental theatre of Bertolt Brecht have appealed to him. Especially repugnant to Genet would have been the Brechtian idea of *Verfremdungseffekt*, or "alienation effect," in which the playwright, with the help of the actors, attempts to make the familiar appear strange, the better to *shatter* illusion so that the audience cannot empathize with any character onstage. The Brechtian audience is not supposed to participate in the drama, it is supposed to cerebrate; that is, Brecht desires the audience to think about what it has seen so that it may learn the lessons set forth in the drama. Brecht feels that, if the audience identifies strongly with the drama, it (the audience) will fall back upon its emotions, not upon its intellect. For Genet, such is not the essence of theatre. We have his own words to the effect that, like Artaud, he feels the audience must be immersed in, not separated from, the metaphysical spectacle that occurs onstage in the theatre in the same way that a communicant is spiritually immersed in a religious ritual. He states this feeling in a letter in which he expresses his intense admiration for the dramatic theories of Artaud, the "Lettre à Pauvert sur *Les Bonnes*," which introduces the J. J. Pauvert edition of *Les Bonnes: Les deux versions précédées d'une Lettre de l'Auteur* (Sceaux, 1954). It is certain, too, that the overt didacticism of Brechtian theatre holds no appeal for Genet, for didacticism holds few, if any, metaphysical implications. On the other hand, the *spectacle* of Brechtian theatre might very easily appeal to him.

Genet's first plays, *Deathwatch* (*Haute Surveillance*)[1] and *The Maids* (*Les Bonnes*), present a kind of progression in technique and idea. They are the least Artaudian of his dramas. Except for their ritualistic presentation and their often exotic use of language, they are rather traditional in presentation. It is into the later dramas, beginning with *The Balcony*, that Genet incorporates much more of Artaud's theory. *Deathwatch* and *The Maids* are, nevertheless, both excellent dramas. Both are as tightly constructed as any classical French tragedy; both take his complex theme of profane play and brilliantly display its many facets; both are well crafted. One might even say of the author's technique that each play is a mirror image of the other. The vaguely homosexual relationship among three men in *Deathwatch* becomes, in *The Maids*, the imperceptibly lesbian relationship among three women.

> "Nobody voluntarily does evil." Certainly: What would you gain? Evil is gratuitous; it is a de luxe activity that demands leisure time and doesn't return anything to the doer. "Crime doesn't pay," they say. And they are right: Evil, like Good, is its own reward.[2]

So says Sartre of evil. It might easily serve as the theme of *Deathwatch*. The drama takes place, naturally enough, in prison. Three handsome young prisoners share the same prison cell, which is the center of the action—Green Eyes ("Yeux-Verts"), a condemned murderer; Lefranc, a soon-to-be-released convict; and Maurice, an effeminate adolescent. The scene opens on an argument between Maurice and Lefranc, in which Green Eyes has intervened. Thus, the triangular relationship among the three men is established. Green Eyes, worshipped as a hero by Maurice, has gratuitously murdered a young woman during a sexual escapade. He is incapable of offering reasons for the murder; it happened in spite of him, against his will. Lefranc admires Green Eyes, but, for him, there is a more awesome presence in the prison, worthier than Green Eyes of veneration—one who is never seen nor heard, but repeatedly mentioned—Snowball ("Boule-de-Neige"), the condemned Negro murderer. Maurice, however, hotly defends Green Eyes as greater than Snowball. The question of which convict is more admirable forms the crux of the conflict between Maurice and Lefranc throughout the play.

The illiterate Green Eyes depends upon Lefranc as his link with the outside world, for Lefranc reads his mail to him and writes letters to his girl for him. But, mistrusting Lefranc, Green Eyes accuses him of attempting to make a play for the girl by making it obvious in the phraseology of the letters that Green Eyes could never have written them. Maurice, seeing a new opportunity to taunt Lefranc, upholds Green Eyes's accusation, and Lefranc is finally goaded into admitting that the accusation is true. However, in so doing, Lefranc traps Maurice into a tacit admission of his homosexual crush on the murderer. While all this has transpired, the girl in question has been waiting in the visitors' room to see Green Eyes, for today, it turns out, is visitors' day, and the guard comes to fetch the murderer. As he converses with Green Eyes, the guard reaches into his pocket, takes out two cigarettes, and gives them to the murderer, explaining that Snowball has sent them as a token of friendship. Green Eyes refuses to see his girl; he gives the guard leave to try his luck with her, and the grateful guard departs.

The friendship between Snowball and Green Eyes surprises both Lefranc and Maurice, and both feel betrayed because of it. Another argument between the two ensues, and Lefranc strangles the boy. Green Eyes, revolted by Lefranc's willful and deliberate murder of Maurice, calls the guard, and the play ends as the cell door unlocks and the guard enters.

It would seem, perhaps, strange that Green Eyes should be so revolted by an act that he himself has also committed until we realize that his act of murder, by his own admission, was not, unlike Lefranc's, willed:

> To blow in casually and bump off a kid! Why . . . I don't even have the heart to mention the name for that sort of criminal. . . . I never knew I was strangling the girl. I was carried away. I didn't want to catch up with anyone. I risked everything and fell flat on my face.
>
> . . . .
>
> You don't know the first thing about misfortune if you think you choose it. I didn't want mine. It chose me. It fell on my shoulders and clung to me. I tried everything to shake it off. . . . [But] it was only when I saw that everything was irremediable that I quieted down. I've only just accepted it. It had to be total. [3]

He has, in short, attained Evil despite himself. As with the great religious saints, his destiny has chosen him, not he, it. He has been "possessed" by Evil and has achieved, as a consequence, a sort of inverse sainthood, and that sainthood is the link between the two convicted murderers. They acquire their status by becoming the playthings of destiny, pawns in the game of Good versus Evil.

The role that Maurice plays in the drama is that of barefoot acolyte at a holy ritual, and Genet quite explicitly indicates in the stage directions that Maurice be barefoot to reinforce the image. An overt homosexual, the boy covets Green Eyes sexually and worships his seemingly complete independence from all people and things. Indeed, the one apparent dependence that Green Eyes has, his dependence upon Lefranc to write his love letters for him, is broken when he gives up his girl to the prison guard. Maurice thinks he perceives in Green Eyes's action of yielding the girl a saintly transcendence of earthly ties. In his eyes, the murderer assumes the proportions of a Promethean hero, entirely alone but completely unbowed and totally indifferent to his fate. But Maurice is betrayed, in a sense, when he discovers the friendship that exists between Snowball and Green Eyes. What has seemed so real to Maurice (i.e., Green Eyes's Promethean apartness and his independence), he now finds to be totally false; he has been trapped by his own illusions concerning his beloved Green Eyes:

> Green Eyes: I'm listening to your charges.
> Maurice: I didn't say anything.
> Green Eyes: Well?
> Maurice: Nothing. I think you've been double-crossing. I realize now that you've always been double-crossing! I've got a right to tell you so because it hurt me just now to discover that you were the black boy's friend. And you didn't let us know.
> Green Eyes: And what if I like to double-cross? Who are you . . . and you? A pair of small-time crooks. It's not the likes of you who can judge me. I look for friends in the prison and I've got a right to. . . .
> Maurice: To me, you're still Green Eyes. A terrific guy. But you've lost your force, your fine criminal force. You belong to your girl more than you realize.[4]

Green Eyes does *not* stand alone; he *has* earthly ties. Therefore, he has lost his force for Maurice. But Maurice is *doubly* betrayed, for he has not understood the import of Green Eyes's relationship with Snowball. The truly criminal are a "chosen people" and form a brotherhood whether they will it or not. They all stand apart; they form a segment of that entity known as Evil, or the Other. As such, Green Eyes is all the worthier of the adoration that Maurice has bestowed upon him, for his "fine criminal force," contrary to being lost, has been merged with the force of all murderers everywhere. Maurice is betrayed then, not only by his illusions concerning Green Eyes, but also by his inability to comprehend the paradox of Green Eyes's worthiness just because of that very betrayal.

If Maurice is the acolyte and Green Eyes the god-like saint in the ritual being enacted onstage, then Lefranc is the high priest of the ceremony. As the priest ingests the god symbolically during the Mass in an attempt to attain the Godhead, so Lefranc attempts to attain Evil through symbolic acts. For instance, he often dons Green Eyes's jacket in an attempt to assume his powers. When acting as Green Eyes's scribe, he"wrote nice letters because *I put myself completely in your place. I got into your skin.*"[5][Italics mine] He also marks himself with a pen to simulate the tatoos of Green Eyes. Maurice, referring to Lefranc's persistent attempts to assume Green Eyes's personality, says of him at one point:

> *Maurice* [to Green Eyes]: Don't ask him anything. Don't ask him anything any more. Can't you see the silly look on his puss? *He's lapping you up. He's gulping you down.*
> *Green Eyes:* Tell me what I'm to do.
> *Maurice:* Just look at that puss of his. He's happy. Everything you say to him sinks right into his skin. *You enter him through his skin and you don't know how you're going to get out. Let him alone.*[6]
> [Italics mine]

Indeed, one might say of Lefranc that he tries to "cannibalize" the essence of Green Eyes right up to the very end of the ritual when, acting as the symbolic high priest, he performs a human sacrifice by strangling Maurice in a deliberate attempt to acquire Green Eyes's "sainthood." If Green Eyes and Snowball have achieved that unholy holiness, criminality, through murder, then why not he, too? But, like Maurice, Lefranc is the victim of a treacherous destiny. Since he has *willed* his crime, since he has chosen it rather than allowing it to choose him, he has failed completely—or so we are led to believe. No inglorious glory, no unholy holiness for him. And he realizes at the end of the play, "I really am all alone!" He is not one of the elect, the "chosen" of Evil, who form a brotherhood because of their unconscious complicity

with Evil. His act is a conscious choice and, consequently, sets him
apart in isolation.

The imagery of the serious "game" of ritual being enacted
onstage is established from the moment the curtains part:

> A prison cell.
> The walls of the cell are of hewn stone and should give the
> impression that the architecture of the prison is very complicated.
> Rear, a barred transom, the spikes of which turn inward. The
> bed is a block of granite on which a few blankets are heaped.
> Right, a barred door.[7]

Very little doubt is left that the cell in which the action occurs
is the tabernacle, the innermost sanctum, of a kind of barbaric
temple of evil repute with its monolithic, rough-hewn walls.
Instead of the usual wooden cots encountered in the ordinary
prison cell, there is a large block of granite; that is, there is an
"altar." It is before this "altar" that Lefranc offers his human sacrifice in vain. The illusion of ritual, moreover, is heightened by
the actors, who "should deaden the timbre of their voices"[8] so
that they almost chant their lines. "The movements of the actors
should be either heavy or else extremely and incomprehensibly
rapid, like flashes of lightning";[9] their movements, in other words,
should be stylized, ritualized. In addition, we are told that the
stage should maintain a hallucinatory, dreamlike quality almost
like that of an early Expressionist film:

> The entire play unfolds as in a dream. The set and costumes . . .
> should be in violent colors. Use whites and very hard blacks,
> clashing with each other. . . .
> . . . .
> Avoid clever lighting. As much light as possible.[10]

The effect the author desires is to bathe the actors and the audience in an aura of illusion, ritual, and nightmare, the better for
them to confront the awesome Presence—or perhaps it would
be more appropriate to speak of the "awesome Absence"—of
Evil. In an Artaudian fashion, he immerses the audience in the
nightmare world of that violence which duplicates the violence
of its own thoughts, a violence which it fearfully refuses to consider a part of itself, but which is as truly a part of itself as its goodness or its benignity.

As a representative of the kind of balancing of opposites that Genet forces on his audience, the prison guard plays an important, though minor, part in the drama. Like all other prison guards, he is, for Genet, the mirror image of the prisoners themselves. Without the guard, the prison, that bastion of Evil, would not be possible, just as, without prisoners, there would be no prison:

> *The Guard:* You don't know what a prison-guard has to see and put up with. You don't realize that he's got to be the very opposite of the thugs. I mean just that: the very opposite. And he's got to be the opposite of their friend. I'm not saying their enemy. Think about it. [11]

The guard, too, like the true criminal, is an instrument of destiny. He does not will his actions: his orders come from "above," and he carries them out impassively, against his will at times. Green Eyes strongly reinforces the impression of the bond linking the prison guard with the prisoner when he makes a present of his girlfriend to the guard:

> *Green Eyes:* Oh, after all, if you like her, try your luck.
> *The Guard:* No kidding? You mean I can?
> . . . .
> *Green Eyes:* You'll talk to her about me. You'll take my place. I'm counting on you to replace me when my head's cut off. [12]

As the prisoner cannot exist without the guard, so the guard cannot exist without the prisoner; each is part of the other. Green Eyes's symbolic gift of his girl to the guard paradoxically insures his own continuity after his death. But, as such, Green Eyes's deed, like so many of his deeds, also constitutes an act of betrayal, for the guard, his opposite, his mirror image, the symbol of society's "good," will become the vehicle of the evil Green Eyes's continuity by accepting the gift.

As in the other dramas, betrayal becomes a game in *Deathwatch*. For instance, the secret and rather playful alliance between Snowball and Green Eyes is tantamount to a betrayal of both Maurice and Lefranc. One of the primary sources of friction between Maurice and Lefranc is each one's contention that his idol is the better—with Maurice, it is Green Eyes; with Lefranc, Snowball. The alliance proves them both wrong, for both idols are, in fact, equal and dependent upon each other; like members of some mystical soccer team, they buttress one another. The alliance, ultimately, is an alliance against Lefranc; it is the alliance of the "real" criminals against the "false" one. Lefranc's name becomes interesting in this connection. It means "the guileless one" or "the frank one." And Lefranc *is* guileless, an absolute innocent in this game of evil, who labors under the gross illusion that he can assume the mantle of evil merely by willing it. After Lefranc's murder of Maurice, Green Eyes quite literally betrays Lefranc to the guard, thus completing the symbolic betrayal begun in the secret alliance between himself and Snowball and "winning" his contest with Lefranc.

At this point, however, a profound ambiguity begins to puzzle the spectator. If complete independence and absolute apartness are the characteristics that are so admired by Lefranc and Maurice in their respective idols until they discover the secret alliance, then has not the outcast Lefranc attained that very independence and apartness by the willful commission of his crime? One is certainly inclined to think so. He who has lost everything—his pending release from prison, his "guilelessness," his illusions concerning Snowball, his attainment of saintly criminality—*wins* in the final analysis. Lefranc comes to the realization that "I really am all alone!" at the end of the play. One imagines that it is a cry of both exultation and despair. He has attained complete Otherness as a contemptible pariah of both the guard's and the criminal's worlds. And he has attained it because of the very illusions that have betrayed him.

Deathwatch was followed by Genet's second drama, *The Maids* (*Les Bonnes*).[13] This second play, like the first, deals with the relationship among three people. In *Deathwatch*, the triangle involves two petty criminals and a murderer; in *The Maids*, two maids and their mistress. But *The Maids* is the first work to move out of the circle of criminals and homosexuals with which all the earlier works, both dramatic and nondramatic, are preoccupied. In this play, we encounter for the first time the bourgeois world, that world of which the criminal world is a mirror image. Moreover, the games and rituals that occur in this drama are no longer circumscribed by the close limits set in *Deathwatch*. No longer set within the confines of the walls of a prison cell as in the first play, the action is now transferred to the framework of a substantial middle-class apartment in Paris. It is part of Genet's evolution as a dramatist that these geographical boundaries move outward as his onstage games take on more cosmic significance—from a prison cell in *Deathwatch* to the apartment in *The Maids* to a nation in the turmoil of revolution in *The Balcony* to the newly awakened continent of Africa in *The Blacks* and, finally, to all of mankind in *The Screens.*

For the first time, too, literal rather than figurative play-acting, masquerade, and impersonation enter Genet's drama and form its most salient features. *The Maids* opens in a sumptuous bedroom:

> Madame's bedroom. Louis-Quinze furniture. Lace. Rear, a window opening on the front of the house opposite. Right, a bed. Left, a door and a dressing table. Flowers in profusion. The time is evening. [14] (p. 35)

Presented with a young matron, ostensibly the bourgeoise proprietress of the house, in the act of dressing, aided by her maid, within moments the audience becomes aware of a jarring and bizarre relationship between mistress and maid: Madame is too cruel and too vituperative; the maid is at once too submissive and too insolent. As the maid advances threateningly on the mistress, an alarm clock rings, and the action stops short for a second. At this point, the audience discovers that everything it has witnessed has been make-believe. Madame is not Madame at all, but the maid Claire impersonating Madame. And the maid who has impersonated Claire is, in reality, Claire's sister Solange. Both women are maids to Madame, and they often engage in these impersonations to express their hatred for Madame, a hatred for which Genet does not furnish any explanation. The two maids clean up the bedroom quickly before Madame's arrival, discussing their situation while they do so.

Both maids have attempted to display their hatred for Madame in more substantial ways, too: Solange by almost strangling her on one occasion when the mistress lay asleep, and Claire by anonymously denouncing Madame's lover to the police, accusing him of some thefts that he had not committed. As a result of

Claire's action, the police have apprehended Monsieur and jailed him; he now telephones to leave a message for Madame to the effect that he has been released for lack of evidence. Consequently, the acts of hate evinced by each of the sisters have miscarried. Solange has drawn back from the murder of Madame at the last moment, and Claire has instituted an abortive scheme against Madame's lover. Claire now hatches a new scheme to rid them of their mistress. The maids will poison Madame's tea that evening. This time, they feel, they will succeed in the murder.

Madame now arrives at home, and, instead of the ogre we might have expected, she is a pretty young bourgeoise who, though haughty and a little silly, seems congenial. Madame is distraught over Monsieur's situation and feels that she should don mourning dress. As a result, she gives a favorite red dress to Claire and a fur cape to Solange. At this point, she notes that the telephone is off its hook; Claire has forgotten to replace it after Monsieur's call. When she asks Claire why it is off the hook, the maid inadvertently mentions Monsieur's call, and Madame, taking the fur cape she has just given to Solange, rushes off to meet him without drinking the poisoned tea.

Now the two sisters take up their impersonations again, and it appears for a brief moment that, offstage, Solange, again masquerading as Claire, may have murdered Claire, who is repeating her impersonation of Madame. But such is not the case, for "Madame" (in reality, Claire) reappears and commands "Claire" (in reality, Solange) to serve her the poisoned tea, which she drinks while her sister delivers the curtain speech.

While the maids' games take place onstage, Genet plays another game with his audience, the game of betrayal again. As *The Maids* begins, the spectator is slowly drawn into the action, fascinated by the apparent relationship between a maid and her mistress. There is nothing onstage to suggest that the two characters are engaged in a masquerade. Then an alarm clock rings and shatters the scene Genet has been building. The spectator is momentarily disoriented until he is able to adjust to the unexpected change. However, he is shaken to such an extent that he remains uneasy until the end of the play, always expecting another abrupt switch in the action. In trying to reveal to his audience a glimpse of the

Evil that it fears so much, Genet secures its attention. Especially when the spectator realizes that he has witnessed a ritual enactment of the maids' innermost evil desires is he forced by Genet to look into the Void of Evil. He is revolted by the author's making a voyeur of him against his will. It is as if he has, unbeknownst to the maids, witnessed them in some loathesome, but compelling, intimate act reserved for the privacy of the boudoir or the privy.

One of the most interesting features of *The Maids* is the prominence given to females. Until this time, women had always played a secondary role in Genet's work. In *Deathwatch*, for instance, the only characters are males. From *The Maids* on, women play major roles—Madame Irma in *The Balcony*; the Queen, Felicity, and Virtue in *The Blacks;* and the Mother, Leïla, and Warda in *The Screens*. But *The Maids* is, in reality, a transitional work in this regard, for Genet desired that adolescent boys play the parts of the maids.

If we reflect for a moment, we are easily able to recall many mythological female figures from various cultures who underscore man's traditional belief in the link between Woman and Evil. For example, there is Lilith, Adam's first wife according to Hebrew tradition, who was banished from Eden for her evil in refusing to submit to him. There are many others: Kali of the Black Tongue, Hindu goddess of death, to whom her followers offered their murder victims as sacrifices; Hecate, Greek goddess of the dark of the moon, whose devotées were adepts at conjuring and at witchcraft; Sekhmet, Egyptian goddess of war; Jezebel, wife of Ahab, whose name has become synonymous with all that is shameless in women; etc., etc. And was it not, after all, Eve who tempted Adam to bring down the curse of God and the loss of Paradise? As for that epitome of perversion and evil, the Black Mass, in which Genet becomes so interested, it too is dominated by women, beginning with its origins in the medieval period. The scholar Jules Michelet[15] expatiates at length upon the role of medieval woman in demonism. The Black Mass, he says, was a "redemption of Eve from the curse Christianity . . . laid upon her." At either of the great semiannual Witches' Sabbaths (October 31 and April 30), woman became the central figure in the demonic ritual. She was the high priestess, profane Host, and vessel of the very God of Evil himself.

It may well be, then, that Genet's meaning in using females lies in the subjugation in which the female has been held in human society. Almost invariably, male society equates femininity with evil, passivity, darkness, and night, and masculinity with good, activity, etc. Genet, by stressing females in important dramatic roles, attempts to reassert all those dark values associated with femininity, without which the daylight masculine world cannot exist (the male-female conflict is discussed at much greater length in chapter 4). Further, by creating quasi-androgynes in *The Maids* —i. e., maids acted by boys—Genet indicates, like the Taoists, that, at heart, all things are one: male and female, good and evil, reality and illusion.

The Maids is, in reality, a prolonged, but interrupted, ritual masquerade—interrupted by the entrance of Madame herself. The interruption, however, is an important one, for it introduces Madame, the focal point of the impersonations, to the audience, and the spectator is consequently able to compare the archetypal, symbolic Mistress of the maids' ritual impersonation with the real mistress. The actual Madame is a shallow, sometimes indulgent, sometimes petulant, but essentially "good" young lady who is saddened over the arrest of her lover. In their play, the maids are better Mesdames than Madame herself, for they become the very essence of mistressdom, with all of its hauteur, its vanity, its pride, and its arrogance. When Madame appears, she is really too sympathetic by half to be an image of the archetypal Mistress. The maids

> are the aristocrats, and Madame is the plebeian symbol espousing only her single image; when she repeats the words that Solange [sic] had previously spoken in her stead, she sounds artificial, as if she were parodying the original. It is the maids who redeem the symbol of Madame by playing her part better than she does, by making her coarse reality a product of art. And this accounts for a part of the maid's hatred: the magnificence which they envy in Madame is of their (spiritual) making.[16]

It is a fault in Madame that she cannot live up to the evil that being a master or a mistress implies. She betrays Claire and Solange in not truly being a mistress; she is not worthy of the monumental hatred lavished by the maids upon her image as it is projected by their masquerades.

When their ritual recommences after Madame's departure, it is brought to a conclusion for the first time since the masquerades began. In their previous impersonations, they had always spent too much time on the preliminaries or on tangential issues to complete the rite before the intrusion of the external, real world in the person of Madame. Now the rite ends as Claire, in the guise of Madame, sacrifices herself. To attain her sacrifice, she demands that her sister pour her a cup of the poisoned tea that had been prepared for Madame—the tea that Madame did not drink before her departure. By her insistence on her sister's complicity in her suicide, Claire forces Solange to complete, at least symbolically, the murder of Madame that Solange, by her own admission, has attempted unsuccessfully to bring herself to accomplish in the past. Solange becomes, as it were, the priestess who performs a ritual murder of a sacrificial victim, much like the ritual murder of Maurice by Lefranc in *Deathwatch*. This suicide-murder of Claire takes on the aura of a monstrous perversion of the play-instinct until we realize the author's intent. Through the sacrifice of the maid, Genet points to illusion as a deeper reality than reality. Both Solange and Claire, in the real world, have been frustrated in their attempts to revenge themselves on Madame either through murder or through attempts to debase her. In the illusory world of their play-activity, however, they are finally able to achieve their goal through the suicide of Claire masquerading as Madame. But on a much deeper level of significance, it is not merely the image of Madame that the maids destroy; they destroy, rather, the very idea of "madameness" itself. Indeed, it seems that the maids have unconsciously insured that the actual Madame will escape their murder plot, for their actions often belie their vituperative remarks. For instance, why does not Claire replace the telephone on its cradle after Monsieur's call? And, instead of lying about the call when questioned by Madame, why does she blurt out all the details of the call in spite of herself? Unless we can impugn a certain clumsiness of plot construction to Genet, we must view Claire's lapses as deliberate devices on the author's part. And such they are. As I have shown, the real Madame is not truly worthy of the name of Mistress; she does not fulfill the archetypal image.

She is not, therefore, worthy of the sacrifice devised by Claire.

When Claire quaffs the poisoned tea, she symbolically destroys the idea of "madameness." In *The Maids*, as in Genet's other works, we are faced with "the reverse-image theme, expressing the absolute interdependence of opposites: servantdom and madameness, the polar complements of each other, must live and die together."[17] In *Deathwatch*, it was noted how opposites depend upon each other for their existence. The prison guard, for example, cannot exist without the prisoner, and Satan cannot exist without God. By the same token, the image of the servant must, of necessity, die with the image of the mistress. The maids symbolize that bondage of the individual to the need for labor, without which our society, as it is presently constructed, cannot survive. The image of the Madame represents the oppressive forces of that work-oriented society. Thus, it becomes doubly significant when, in the illusory world of play, Madame is symbolically killed. Genet declares to all who would listen that domination in a work-oriented society can be abolished only in the re-creative world of imagination and play. It is only in a world where the imagination is given free play to be on a totally equal footing with the reality principle, not subordinated to it, that complete freedom is achieved and servantdom is abolished. Those who are forced to serve the reality principle (as the maids are) are doubly prisoners—prisoners of their lot in the real world and prisoners of their illusions. But, paradoxically, their imprisonment in illusion is their only freedom, their only escape from an oppressive reality. In the absence of the absolute freedom to play, they must, to maintain their freedom, surrender to imprisonment in the playful world of imagination and illusion.

Both the early dramas succeed in establishing an equilibrium between the playful world of illusion and the inhibiting world of reality. The author achieves that equilibrium by allowing a primacy to the world of play that it has rarely, if ever, achieved in the world of reality. What Genet indicates to his audiences is that his major characters, Lefranc, Solange, and Claire, achieve an inverse salvation only when they enter into *worlds of their own devising* to achieve a magnificent isolation—much as children might do in their more fanciful daydreams.

3 | THE
BALCONY

In *Querelle of Brest*, Madame Lysiane is the proprietress of La Feria, a unique bordello in which clients may enact their most secret sexual fantasies. It is the sort of bordello that serves as the scene of Genet's third drama, *The Balcony* (*Le Balcon*)—a drama that, despite its flawed sixth scene, easily ranks among the best of the twentieth century. As the drama opens, a revolution rages outside the bordello. Roger, one of the leaders of the revolution, has succeeded in smuggling Chantal, one of the prostitutes, out of the bawdyhouse.

In the first scene, we are confronted with a mock Bishop, dressed and made up larger than life (as are all the patrons), who has listened to the confession of a mock-penitent whore as a prelude to the sex act. Since he has used up all of his allotted time and more, Mme. Irma, the owner of the establishment, enters the studio to urge him to leave so that it may be prepared for the next guest. After some procrastination, the Bishop disrobes, dons his street clothes, and departs. The next scene presents a sadomasochistic pseudo-Judge dealing out punishment to a female Thief with the aid of a mock Executioner. As the scene closes, the Judge debases himself, crawling on the floor before the Thief. A would-be General dominates the third scene: the harlot in the tableau acts the part of his horse. And in the fourth, and briefest, scene a mock Tramp obtains his masochistic pleasures from a whip-wielding prostitute.

During the next scene, which involves Madame Irma and the sexually impotent Chief of Police, we find that the Chief longingly awaits the day when he can join the Nomenclature; that is, the day when a brothel customer requests a game in which he can impersonate the Chief. The scene shifts next to the revolutionaries in the square outside the bordello, who decide, against Roger's wishes, that Chantal shall become a symbol for the revolution. The revolution thereafter ostensibly succeeds in dispatching most of the important members of the government. But a government Envoy persuades Mme. Irma and the customers who have masqueraded as Bishop, as Judge, and as General to assume respectively the roles of the Queen and of church and governmental officials. Consequently, the revolution is squelched by the Chief of Police after "Queen" Irma and her entourage show themselves to the people, who had believed these symbols of authority dead. Subsequently, Roger arrives at The Grand Balcony (the bordello), asking for a game in which he can assume the role of the Chief of Police, who can now be inscribed in the Nomenclature. During his impersonation of the Chief, however, Roger castrates himself. And the Chief of Police himself descends into a crypt. At this point, a revolution breaks out again, and the play ends as Mme. Irma dismisses the audience from the theatre.

Play and illusion form the heart of *The Balcony*. Genet says, in "Comment Jouer *Le Balcon*," which introduces the final edition of the play, published in 1961:

> The feelings of the protagonists inspired by the situation —are they fake? Are they real? The anger of the Chief of Police toward the Three Great Figures near the end of the play—is it fake? Is it real? Is the existence of the revolutionaries inside or outside the bordello? It is necessary to hold to this ambiguity to the end. [1]

No doubt can remain, therefore, that the author desires to evoke in the spectator a certain ambivalence concerning illusion and reality, and he reinforces this ambivalence in his stage directions for the first scene of the play:

> On the right wall, a mirror, with a carved gilt frame, reflects an unmade bed which, if the room were arranged logically, would be in the first rows of the orchestra. [2] (p. 1)

The same mirror reflects the same unmade bed in the next two scenes. Through this subtle Artaudian device at the beginning of the drama, the audience is implicated in the games played in Mme. Irma's studios. At the end of the play, Mme. Irma turns to the audience and addresses it directly:

> [Soon] I'll have to start all over again . . . put all the lights on again . . . dress up. . . . (She stops in the middle of the stage, facing the audience). . . . You must now go home, where everything—you can be quite sure—*will be even falser than here* [Italics mine]. . . . You must go now. You'll leave by the right, through the alley. . . . (She extinguishes the last light.) It's morning already.[3] (p. 114)

The confusion between reality and illusion is made quite explicit by Genet in the above scenes. First, through the clever use of mirrors, he involves us completely in the illusory play-world of the bordello, which is really a game within a game within a game; that is, the drama itself is a game in which actors take the roles of gasmen, plumbers, and bankers, who, in turn, play at being bishops, generals, and judges in The Grand Balcony. Then, the game becomes "reality" as the revolution forces the mock Bishop, the mock Judge, the mock General, and "Queen" Irma to appear before the people as the authentic personages. And, finally, the game becomes a game again as the revolution subsides and the characters revert to their original roles as prosaic workmen and businessmen, at which point, speaking directly from the stage, the world of illusion, Mme. Irma tells the audience to return to the real world where things are "falser than here." The real world *is* falser than illusion because of the nature of "reality," which is no more than the masks imposed upon the individual by society; that is, all the roles that he is forced to play in his lifetime (in a Pirandellian sense)—father, husband, lover, plumber, uncle, etc.—probably none of which truly express his innermost reality, the Self. Beware then of the "real" world, Genet says, because there is no hard and fast line between it and the world of the imagination. At the point where the two worlds merge, each obscures the other. Just as the real world is based in illusory, transitory roles that we play (son, student, friend, brother), so the world of our fantasies is colored by reality, for in fantasy we assume roles that we covet in the real world. Lefranc in *Death-*

watch, for instance, in his fantasies, dreams of becoming a murderer like Green Eyes and Snowball. When he attempts to turn his fantasies into actuality by murdering Maurice, he forces the worlds of illusion and reality to merge, and he seemingly loses everything—his illusions about what constitutes true criminality, his impending release from prison, his very life. Green Eyes, symbol of the fearful world of illusion and death, loathes him, and so does the prison guard, symbol of the real world. He has, then, apparently lost both worlds. *But*, in "losing," Lefranc actually wins. By having attained the realm where reality and illusion become integrated into a whole, he achieves a sort of inverse godhead—an absolute isolation from all others. Likewise, Claire and Solange enter this integral world and achieve their freedom at the end of *The Maids* when the false Claire murders the false Madame; that is, again, when the world of the masquerade and the dream-wish is made to coincide with the everyday world. And I will show later that the Chief of Police, too, achieves a splendid apotheosis when he synthesizes the two worlds. As a matter of fact, it is to the propensity to assume "real" roles when we fantasize that the whorehouse in the drama owes its existence.

To perpetuate the impact on the viewer of the world where reality and illusion become confused, *The Balcony* depends heavily on its decor. Throughout the first three scenes, the set remains essentially unchanged—the same mirror reflecting an unmade bed, the same chandelier overhead—except for three large screens, which are changed to indicate movement from the masquerade in one studio to the masquerade in the next. The red screens indicating a sacristy in the Bishop's scene become the Judge's brown screens, which are transformed, in turn, into the General's green screens. These screens become important in any discussion of reality and illusion in the drama because they indicate Genet's growing preoccupation with the ambiguous nature of both states. With moveable screens, reality can be altered, hidden, or exaggerated to create a sense of illusion. [4] To heighten the sense of ambiguity concerning the shifting levels of reality and illusion, Genet designates that the place of the three screens of the first three scenes be taken by three mirrors—which are not mirrors at all—in the fourth scene:

A room, the three visible panels of which are three mirrors in
which is reflected a little old man, dressed as a tramp. . . .
. . . .
All the gestures of the little old man are reflected in the three
mirrors. (Three actors are needed to play the roles of the reflections.) [5] (p. 24)

Mirrors, symbolic of illusion, become empty frames containing
real actors impersonating the reflections of an old man who acts
out a fantasy. There can be no doubt that the author intends a
confusion between the two worlds. It is as if he were suggesting
that no clear, marked delineation between the "day" world of
reality, work, and pragmatism, and the "night" world of illusion,
play, and dream exists; there is, rather, a gradual transition through
either a murky twilight or a hazy dawn from one world to the
other. And it is in this indistinct *demi-monde* that the action of *The
Balcony* occurs.

Genet again illustrates the confusion between illusion and
reality when the impersonators of highly placed personages are
forced by circumstances to assume the roles of the authentic figures
whom they have impersonated; and they become, for a time,
quite literally, imprisoned in their dream-roles. And again Genet's
paradox proliferates almost endlessly. But can these figures
be considered "real" after all? Genet intensifies the paradox
when the fake Bishop, the fake Judge, the fake General, and the
fake Queen, having now become "real," defeat the revolution-
ists, those supposed enemies of illusion (and of Mme. Irma's
"house of illusions"), who are routed by the appearance of figures
whom they thought dead—by the appearance, that is, of "real"
personages who are not real at all. And so the realistic revolution-
ists are defeated by illusion, but only temporarily, for a revolution soon breaks out again—as it must to maintain the proper relationship between the two worlds.

Notwithstanding the confusion that exists between illusion and
reality in *The Balcony*, Genet signifies his preference for the regions of illusion, play, and imagination, primarily, perhaps, to
reassert their importance in a world that is too reality-oriented.
Each of the clients' impersonations witnessed at the beginning of
the drama is a deadly serious affair despite its play-nature, even

for the harlots. Irma says, at one point, "I don't allow any joking. . . . A smile means doubt. The clients want sober ceremonies. My house is a severe place"[6] (p. 27).

Each of the customers of the bordello dresses in an exaggerated costume and wears cothurni during the enactment of his fantasy. In addition to the suggestion of ritual, these outsize costumes and tall shoes also connote children at play—a little girl in mother's dress, a little boy in his father's top hat and dinner jacket, both seriously involved in the game of being grown-up. This association of ideas is confirmed by the identities of the people impersonating high officials, for these are, in fact, men of small power outside the brothel. As with children's play-activity, if a man is to "play" a role, that role should live up to his illusion of it; it should be larger than life. It should lie in the realm of the unattainable just as the children's aping of the adult world does. The use of the cothurni and the outlandish costumes also emphasizes the theatricality of what occurs onstage, thereby reinforcing the spectator's perception of the illusory aspect of the onstage games and, ultimately, of the drama itself.

It is significant that *The Balcony* opens with the Bishop. Bishops concern themselves with matters of ritual, and ritual becomes a central feature of the play. As with the maids' impersonations in *The Maids*, each of the games witnessed in *The Balcony* follows a ritualistic pattern. Indeed, Genet himself suggested that the entire play be performed as if it were a solemn Mass in a cathedral. The ritual of the Mass might be termed Artaudian in its ability to evoke a collective response in the celebrants (who, incidentally, are called *participants in the Holy Sacrifice of the Mass*). And "for Genet the greatest metaphors and the highest form of ceremony are to be found in the Mass: 'Beneath the familiar appearance—a crust of bread—a god is devoured. I know of nothing more theatrically effective than the elevation of the host. . . .' "[7] Moreover, the Mass also unifies its participants in a mystical sense of belief, and it is exactly this kind of union that Genet seeks in his theatre.[8] It is precisely this metaphysical union of his audience that he hopes to achieve through his use of ritual, not only in *The Balcony*, but in all his dramas.

These serious ritual games in the bordello satisfy all the requisites for play. For example, fun and games in the whorehouse are circumscribed spatially and temporally; they are indulged in voluntarily and seriously, and they are limited by a set of rules.[9] The rules, as a matter of fact, are spelled out on various occasions by the game-participants:

> *The Judge:* . . . Look here: you've got to be a model thief if I'm to be a model judge. If you're a fake thief, I become a fake judge. Is that clear?
> *The Thief:* Oh yes, your Honor.
> *The Judge* (He continues reading): Good. Thus far everything has gone off well. My executioner has hit hard . . . for he too has his function. We are bound together, you, he, and I. For example, if he didn't hit, how could I stop him from hitting? Therefore, he must strike so that I can intervene and demonstrate my authority. And you must deny your guilt so that he can beat you.[10] (p. 11)

The main character in *The Balcony* is Mme. Irma, the proprietress of the "maison d'illusions," which she governs as a "mistress of the games," so to speak. Irma is Genet himself in "drag," for she speaks with his voice. He, too, is the *magister ludi*, the unseen director of the action, who creates a masterful illusion onstage for the audience, implicating it deeply in the games being played, taunting it with visions it really does not want to see, and assaulting it with insights it does not desire to comprehend. Irma participates in the fantasy-games not only as directress, but also as a voyeur, stationing herself periodically at a television outlet connected with each of the studios. Through this device, Irma is able to hold the illusory world of games somewhat under her control. It is appropriate that Irma engage in this kind of voyeurism, for her action attests to her symbolic role as the *Absence* that presides over all the rituals of death and illusion enacted in the studios of the brothel. Illusion, which forms the core of the play-activity in each of the studios, is also an Absence in that it is not real, nonexistent; since it is a state of nonbeing, it may be equated with stasis and death. And yet, illusion is the most important single element in any game. It is interesting, in this light, to note the connection between orgasm and death, a connection made explicit in the Elizabethan era, when fornication was euphemized as "dying"; each of the games in The Grand Balcony, of course, ends in such a "death." As if to reinforce the imagery of Irma as a personification of illusion and death, Genet designates in "Comment Jouer *Le Balcon*" that:

> It goes without saying that Irma's costume, at the beginning of the play, should be very austere. *One can even imagine her in mourning.* [Italics mine] It is in the scene with Carmen that she dresses less austerely, wearing the long dress that, in the Balcony Scene, will become, thanks to a few decorations, the dress of the Queen. [11]

In other words, during the course of the drama, Irma exchanges a quasi-mourning costume for a shroudlike dress in her dead world. Even the prostitutes must be sterile and, consequently, figuratively "dead" in the illusory world of play:

> *Irma* [speaking of her whores]: How can I call you, *my long sterile girls? They never fertilize you,* [Italics mine] and still . . . if you weren't there? [12]

As adumbrated in the last question in the speech, if the whores, connoting the world of illusion, were not there, how could the "real" life of the external world be supported? Probably not at all. The necessary tension between reality on the one hand and illusion, imagination, and play on the other would dissipate; yet, the one depends on the other for its life. It is, as a matter of fact, when this tension dissolves that the "real" world of the revolution is defeated—in which context Chantal becomes meaningful.

The sixth scene of the revised edition of the drama, which deals with Roger, Chantal, and the revolutionaries, is flawed by its illusionary character. In the original edition of the play, the author keenly highlighted the anti-illusion, anti-play character of the revolution, posing it against the playful world of the bordello. It was more effective both aesthetically and technically than the dreamlike atmosphere and the poetic language that is encountered in the revised sixth scene. One is hard put to comprehend why Genet felt constrained to change the scene so drastically, since the first edition, though not perfect, worked so well.

Chantal has been spirited away from Irma's "maison d'illusions" by Roger, a leader of the revolution, who attempts to make her over into a rational realist. Roger and the revolutionaries are "by definition the ones who don't play; they are . . . the reality of their action. The brothel is their symbolic enemy. . . . These priests of factuality are solemn. . . . the moment their action takes on the appearance of a game, they will find themselves defeated even in victory, having merely replaced the old order by another image of itself."[13] Soon the revolutionary leaders decide that Chantal will become a symbol for the revolution, a move that Roger, the realist, opposes.

Roger, in Chantal's words, has "snatched her from a grave";[14] that is, from the "death" that is the world of illusion in the brothel. Now she will symbolically reenter that world with her assumption of the play-role of the "Soul of the Revolution"; it is a world into which Roger cannot follow her. And so Chantal, one of Mme. Irma's former "longues stériles," a creature from the world of play and illusion, becomes the symbol of the insurrection. When the realistically inclined revolution accepts Chantal as a symbol, it resorts to illusion and imagination, and, in so doing, it defeats itself. Having accepted one illusion, Chantal, the insurgents easily accept another, "Queen" Irma, and with that acceptance comes the death of the revolution, the world of reality. Reality, however, soon reasserts itself as a revolution (perhaps the same one?) commences again after Chantal's death and Irma's reversion to procuress. As for the real Queen, about whose existence the Envoy is quite indefinite, stating only that she is away embroidering, we may assume that she reascends the throne when Irma returns to the bordello.

Perhaps the most interesting character in *The Balcony* is the Chief of Police, Georges. His role is the most ambiguous one in the play. Georges is the principal link between the brothel and the real world outside it. Although he desires it mightily, the Chief of Police cannot enter the play-world of the bordello completely because he is not listed in the Nomenclature; no clients have ever asked to play his role in one of the studios as they have requested games involving the roles of Bishop, Judge, or General. In Mme. Irma's Nomenclature are inscribed all the roles in Western Society that have attained the status of archetypes; i.e., roles that men wish to imitate. They are roles that have existed for millenia, and men have, for a long period, held them in awe, for they are images removed from the masses of people—and this is true for the image of the Tramp as well as for the image of the General. Since they are inaccessible to the ordinary man in the work-a-day world, these images generate an irresistible aura of romance to which men are invariably drawn. The Chief of Police has not entered the Nomenclature because his archetypal function, unlike those of the Church, the Law, the Government, and the Military, has yet to be discovered (though it has existed for a long time, as I will presently show). The images of Bishop, Queen, Judge, Tramp, Saint, General, etc., can draw upon thousands of years of accrued tradition. They are historic roles that men, unhappy in their assigned roles, have consciously aspired to. However, they are roles in which the actual personages portraying them are as unhappy as the men who aspire to them. This fact is amply illustrated when the fake Bishop, the fake Judge, and the fake General become "real":

> *The Bishop:* Very well. Then we shall go back to our rooms and there continue the quest of an absolute dignity. For we were content there, and it was you who came and dragged us away. . . . You tore us brutally from that delicious, enviable, untroubled state. . . .
> *The General* (interrupting the Bishop): My breeches! What joy when I pulled on my breeches! I now sleep in my general's breeches. . . . I live in my general's breeches. I'm a general the way one is a priest.
>
> . . . .
> . . . I used to start a month in advance!—prepare myself for pulling on my general's boots and breeches. Now I'm rigged in them for all eternity. By Jove, I no longer dream.
> *The Bishop* (to the Chief of Police): *You see, he no longer dreams* [Italics mine]. Our ornamental purity, our luxurious and barren—and sublime—appearance has been eaten away.[15]
> (pp. 95–96)

The General is unable to dream any longer because his fantasies have been fulfilled too suddenly; he cannot adjust to a dream so quickly turned into reality. Consequently, he exists only in the world of a newly acquired reality now—a reality far less glamorous than his dream-world of play and impersonation. Man can be happy only in his dreams, even if those dreams are drawn from misapprehensions concerning the role he desires in the real world. This is true, too, both of Lefranc in *Deathwatch* and of the maids in *The Maids*. When dreams suddenly become totally real, they become stifling, tiresome, and disillusioning after a time. No position in the real world can satisfy a man once he has achieved it; he always dreams of another, more desirable position in that world when he has attained a role he has dreamed about for a long time. The role of the Chief of Police is to mediate between the worlds of dream and reality, but not only does he mediate between the two worlds, he also inhabits each. And because he is able to inhabit each, he, like Lefranc, is able to attain a synthesis of the two worlds. Because of his achievement, he can retain a certain amount of control over each world. Like Lefranc again, both worlds despise him. As if in revenge against him for the hate and fear he inspires, the populace does not respond to his image with the same imitative lust that it showers upon the glamorous, long established archetypes. His archetypal function has yet to be discovered.

But what exactly is that function? To answer that question, a roundabout route must be taken, pausing at one of the most crucial scenes in *The Balcony*, the scene in which Roger, masquerading as the Chief of Police in the bordello, castrates himself. Martin Esslin signifies that Roger's "act of self-castration while impersonating the Police Chief is an ambivalent one; he wants to punish himself for his desire for power, and at the same time punish the Police Chief vicariously by an act of sympathetic magic."[16] Lionel Abel, in his *Metatheatre*, designates the castration episode as "brutal, vulgar, and utterly undramatic."[17] Esslin's explanation of the mutilation seems altogether too simple to apply to work of a playwright like Genet, who delights in the paradox, for it fails to take into account too many factors. For instance, why should the castration occur when the Chief of Police has finally achieved his long desired inclusion in the Nomenclature? Certainly, the Chief's subsequent apotheosis is inexplicable within Esslin's framework. Abel's statement, on the other hand, seems rather imperceptive; the mutilation scene *does* have a strong dramatic—and metaphysical—impact on the audience. Indeed, it comes about as close as one can to *pure* Artaudian theatre.

Robert Brustein probably comes closer to Genet's intent when he analyzes Roger's act of castration during his impersonation of the Chief of Police. The castration, he says, proves the divinity of the Chief of Police, "for mutilation is the destiny of the Man-God, whether he be Christ, Osiris, or Dionysus."[18] Brustein maintains that the mutilation bestows godhead upon the Chief of Police, for, like the ancient gods, "he has been mutilated and remained whole; like them, he has been imitated, and will continue to be imitated."[19]

To return to the question, what exactly is the function conceived by the Chief of Police that finally makes him an archetypal figure? That function is the fusion of reality and illusion (which is reflected in the ambiguous nature of the two realms throughout the drama), of work and play, of life and death, of time and timelessness, of the conscious and the unconscious into a harmonious and awesome unity—into a kind of immortality. But it is not the kind of immortality that implies a flight from death; it is rather the acceptance of death as a *continuity*. To elucidate this notion of death as continuity, the analogy that Georges Bataille uses in his *Death and Sensuality* can be employed. Bataille points to the union of the sperm with the egg to form the zygote; each cell has died (i.e., lost its individual nature), yet continues in the new cell:

> Sperm and ovum are, to begin with, discontinuous entities, but they *unite*, and consequently a continuity comes into existence between them to form a new entity from the death and disappearance of the separate beings. The new entity is itself discontinuous, but it bears within itself the transition to continuity, the fusion, fatal to both, of two separate beings.[20]

He says elsewhere:

> Mankind conspires to ignore the fact that death is also the youth of things. Blindfolded, we refuse to see that only death

guarantees the fresh upsurging without which life would be blind. We refuse to see that life is the trap set for the balanced order, that life is nothing but instability and disequilibrium. Life is a swelling tumult continuously on the verge of explosion. But since the incessant explosion constantly exhausts its resources, it can only proceed under one condition: that beings given life whose explosive force is exhausted shall make room for fresh beings coming into the cycle with renewed vigor.[21]

Viewed in this light, the castration scene takes on even more cogent and complex significance. It manifests an attempt to become the father, symbol of the generation that must expire (that is, become *continuous*, attain the state of nonbeing) in order to insure the survival of the succeeding generation (which is *discontinuous*; that is, whose individuals are distinct from one another). When the Chief of Police's alter ego, Roger, mutilates himself, he reenacts the myth of the castration of Ouranos by his son Kronos (whose name, of course, means *time*). In this drama, however, unlike the myth, castrator and castrated are the same person. Thus, in *The Balcony*, the symbolic castrated being becomes not only father, but also son, actor and receptor, at the same time; he is life and death at once, and, as I will show, he is man and woman at once. When, immediately after his alter ego's castration, the Chief of Police checks his impotent phallus to discover whether it is still in place, he strengthens the imagery, for he too is at once symbolically alive and dead. His phallus, "giver" of life, is forever detumescent, "dead." Likewise, as Genet's plot indicates, he descends into permanent *entombment* to insure his immortality: as he unites reality and illusion within his person, so too he unites life and death. By the same token, he requests that his image be a giant phallus carved from rock, the huge, fertile, life giving symbol of the phallus united forever with the sterile, dead rock.

The castration also symbolizes an attempt to re-create the the state of blissful childhood before a tyrannical society has imposed its rules. In this regard, the act may be seen as an assertion of the androgynous principle:

> Infantile sexuality . . . just because it is infantile, must be sexually undifferentiated; and since the structure of infancy is

the same for both sexes, the basic demands of the libido are the same for both sexes.[22]

In other words, the castration is tantamount to a rejection of an oppressive, genitally-oriented culture and an affirmation of childhood's sexually undifferentiated state—that is to say, bisexuality. The genital organization of society with its

> subordination of fore-pleasure to end-pleasure in sexual intercourse is a compromise concealing a conflict between the desire of the immortal child in us for pure polymorphous play and the reality principle which imposes genital organization on us. This conflict explains that while it is not true, as the Church father said, that *post coitum omne animal triste*, it is true of the human animal: the immortal child in us is frustrated, even in the sexual act, by the tyranny of genital organization.[23]

When the symbolic castration occurs, the Chief of Police attains more than mere inclusion in the Nomenclature; he attains apotheosis. The apotheosis denotes not only the historic continuity of the new image of play, but also the transcendence of the "immortal child" beyond play—his assumption of the powers of Godhead to generate a whole new cycle of history.

The Balcony, perhaps more than any other twentieth-century Western drama—with the exception of *The Blacks*—may be best characterized by the Taoist symbol that opens this work. The dramatic piece incorporates brilliantly all the disparate elements of *play* into its imagery—the *impersonations* of the bordello clients, the *illusions* of the revolutionaries, the *ritualized* sexual ministrations of the whores, the *mythic* implications of the Chief of Police, and the *negation* of our genitally-oriented society—to indicate Genet's now fully developed thesis of the autonomous nature of the "dark" side of the human psyche, which is, at once, independent of the "light" side and curiously dependent upon it. It is his recognition of this ambiguous autonomy and interdependence of "dark" and "light" that crystallizes in the bisexual nature of the Chief of Police at the end of the drama, who becomes an ecstatically transcendent figure.

4 | THE BLACKS*

After *The Balcony*, Genet presented *The Blacks* (*Les Nègres*), which is, in all probability, the dramatic masterpiece of contemporary theatre. As the reader peruses *The Blacks*—or, more tellingly, as the audience watches the play—two startling facts begin to emerge. First, the play was conceived in France by a French author, and second, it was written in 1960; yet, it has far greater relevance in the contemporary United States than it had in the France of the early sixties. And for that reason, it overshadows all his other work. *The Blacks* deals with the rancor of blacks against whites; it vibrates with black vituperation and hatred—so much so that the spectator must remind himself repeatedly that a white formulated the ingredients for this drama.

The drama commences as a group of blacks, dressed in "le plus grand mauvais goût," performs an elegantly precise minuet around a draped catafalque. As they dance, five black impersonators of important white personages enter on a raised platform to view the proceedings. They wear white masks and are costumed to represent a Queen, her Valet, a Missionary, a Judge, and a military colonial Governor.[1] The minuet ends and Archibald, the master of ceremonies, introduces each of the blacks to the court of "whites" behind him and to the audience in front of him; the blacks are to reenact the rape-murder of a white woman, a ritual that they execute every evening. Before they launch into the ritual, however, Archibald dismisses Edgar Hélas Ville de

---

* A condensation of this chapter appeared as "Myth, Magic, and Play in Genet's *The Blacks*," in *Contemporary Literature*, Vol. XI, No. 4 (© 1970 by the Regents of the University of Wisconsin), pp. 511–525.

Saint-Nazaire (called "Newport News" in the American ver-
sion of the play) from the stage to fulfill a commitment—a commitment, it turns out, to assist in the trial and execution of a
black traitor offstage. It seems that the blacks are clandestinely
devising an antiwhite revolution in the outside world. Ville de
Saint-Nazaire appears at intervals during the onstage performance
to inform the actors of the progress of events "outside."

The ritualized rape finally begins when Diouf, a complaisant
black, assumes the role of a white female as he envelops himself
in a blonde wig, white mask, and voluminous skirt. Village,
acting as the black rapist, leaves the side of Virtue, a black whore
whom he loves, and proceeds to seduce the symbolic white
woman, but not before five white dolls (representing the figures
of the court) are retrieved from beneath her skirt and hung on the
raised platform. After his "seduction" and "rape" of the representative white female, Village "murders" her. Now the
white court attempts to avenge the murder by coming down from
its raised platform into "Africa"; i.e., into the midst of the
blacks. One by one, the members of the court are symbolically
assassinated by the blacks as a cock crows. Village then returns to
Virtue as all the blacks, including those who have impersonated
whites (now without their masks), exit behind a black backdrop,
and the two lovers exchange words of love. The backdrop rises
as they speak, and all the blacks who have left the stage are
gathered about the same white catafalque that was in the center of
the stage as the play opened. They perform the same mock-
elegant minuet as before to the strains of music from Mozart's
Don Giovanni. Village and Virtue join in the dance as the play
ends. [2]

In *The Blacks*, the world of death, obscenity, criminality,
perversity, illusion, and betrayal is celebrated by Genet as if he
were the chief, albeit invisible, priest at a demonic ritual. And,
as in *The Balcony*, he suffuses that world with an atmosphere
of play-acting, impersonation, and fantasy. There are, indeed,
many parallels that can be drawn between *The Balcony* and
The Blacks, even though the latter play represents a more complex,
multifaceted, and deeper world view. Take, for instance, the
Artaudian implication of the audience in the drama. At the outset

of *The Balcony*, the audience becomes involved in the erotic occurrence onstage through the subtle use of a mirror to reflect an unmade bed, which, if logically placed, would be in the audience. And, as if to insure that the audience will not leave the theatre at the end of the drama to forget its metaphysical complicity in what has happened, Genet causes Mme. Irma to address the audience directly in such a fashion as to leave no doubt in its mind of its implication in what it has just witnessed. In *The Blacks*, Genet's technique of eliciting the audience's complicity is at once more direct and more subtle than in the earlier drama:

> This play . . . is intended for a white audience, but if, which is unlikely, it is ever performed before a black audience, then a white person . . . should be invited every evening. The organizer of the show should welcome him formally, dress him in ceremonial costume and lead him to his seat, preferably in the front row of the orchestra. The actors will play for him. A spotlight should be focused upon this symbolic white throughout the performance.[3](p. 4)

Obviously, Genet means for the white audience really to be at the center of the action of *The Blacks* in order better to receive the vituperation and contempt heaped upon it. Out of the blacks' hatred and contempt grows a spectacle in which these modern black buffoons, like the fool in *King Lear*, entertain the Queen, her entourage, and the white audience with posturings, jokes, and shows. The Five Great Figures—and, by extension, the audience—are unable to perceive that these clowns are "more knave than fool," mocking them and, in mocking them, showing them some devastating truths about themselves. Antonin Artaud himself could not have formulated a better dramatic vision of metaphysical cruelty. Moreover, at the beginning of the play, the directions signify that Archibald salute both the Court and the audience, "s'adressant tantôt au public, tantôt à la Cour."[4] And, at various times during the performance, he addresses his remarks directly to the spectators *and* the Court. Thus, a symbolic equation between the masked members of the Court and the audience is established. At one point in the action, a spectator is summoned from the auditorium directly to the stage in order, ostensibly, to hold the knitting of Diouf, who is masquerading as the white woman later "murdered." Actually, the spectator onstage acts as a surrogate for the entire white audience in order to witness a symbolic birth, which becomes important in any understanding of *The Blacks*.

The black actors in the Black Mass enacted onstage are sacred chalices, vehicles of the God of Evil, the "black" god; it is they who convey the lyricism of the world of darkness to the communicants in the rite. The members of the audience, as communicants, are implicated in the ceremony, willingly or unwillingly, and are finally drawn into Genet's resplendently evil world—a world that, on the "outside," as members of a reality-oriented, white-centered, "good" society, they are intent upon destroying, but a world by which they are, nevertheless, secretly fascinated. Upon entering the playwright's world, they are faced with a fearful fact: this exotic, inverted world of illusion is more compelling than the familiar, secure, drab world of the established order. It is in these precincts that Genet assaults his audience, ravishes it, and revels in his assault as an act of saintliness; he has succeeded in injuring his injurers, in betraying his betrayers. And he is able figuratively to address each member of the audience in the words of one of his lineal spiritual ancestors, Baudelaire: *"Hypocrite lecteur!—mon semblable,—mon frère!"*

The Blacks is a playfully conceived, playfully presented ritual of hatred, betrayal, and violence directed against "Whiteness." And whiteness, for Genet, represents (as it does in the Taoist cosmology) "good," light, day, life, work, reality, masculinity, activity, etc. But, as in the Taoist cosmological symbol, the whiteness contains a kernel of blackness at its core just as the blackness that composes the other half of the revolving circle and represents the opposites of all the traits mentioned above contains a kernel of whiteness at its core. The two opposing attributes are, therefore, inseparably bound together—though now one, now the other may be in the ascendancy. Genet indicates this inseparability of black and white in his betrayal even of the black actors in the play. When all is ended, Genet the traitor betrays his actors as he causes the Five Great Figures to be unmasked before us as blacks. Moreover, the audience knows that Ville de Saint-

Nazaire (Newport News) is only an actor after all and that there has been no black revolution going on behind the scenes—no trial and execution of a black traitor in which he is supposedly a key figure. The dramatist has further played the traitor with the blacks because of his cyclical vision of history, represented by the minuet with which the play opens and closes. To be sure, the crowing of cocks as the Great Figures are "killed" symbolizes the dawning of a new day for the blacks, but the Queen indicates in her final speech that a resurgence of whites will occur at some time in the future, when the blacks become as effete as the whites presently are.

Whiteness, besides representing "good," light, day, etc., also means for Genet—and this may represent its kernel of blackness—hypocrisy and repression. The hypocrisy is the "masking" of the Self to present a series of various facades to conform to the standards imposed by the outside world (an idea that *The Balcony* also illustrates). The repression implied in whiteness is the repression of the "black" unconscious, the region of dream, illusion, and play. This hypocritical, repressive aspect of whiteness becomes apparent from the moment the Court enters the stage:

> Each actor playing a member of the Court is a masked Negro whose mask represents the face of a white person. The mask is worn in such a way that the audience sees a wide black band all around it, and even the actor's kinky hair.[5] (p. 8)

Since the white audience is equated with the "white" Court (see above), Genet thus intimates the essential "blackness" of all whites underneath the façades that they present to the world. "Blackness" is repressed in the "white" daylight world of consciousness and reality and dominated by that world just as the blacks are dominated by whites:

> Archibald: When we leave this stage, we are involved in your life. I am a cook, this lady is a sewing-maid, this gentleman is a medical student, this gentleman is a curate at St. Anne's, this lady . . . skip it. Tonight, our sole concern will be to entertain you.[6] (p. 14)

In *The Balcony*, gasmen, plumbers, and bankers come to the

whorehouse to fantasize and play-act roles different from those they play in real life. In *The Blacks*, black cooks, medical students, and vicars come to the stage to play-act roles, too. In both dramatic works, characters attempt to express repressed longings through their play activities. But repressed "blackness" reasserts itself explosively at the end of *The Blacks* as the "white" Queen declares before her "death":

> How I have loved! And now I die—I must confess—choked by my desire for a Big Black Buck. Black nakedness, thou hast conquered me.[7] (p. 124)

Blacks live in a white world, but whites secretly desire the black world. Even if blackness conquers today, however, it contains that bit of whiteness that will gain force with the passage of time and reconquer ten thousand years hence:

> *The Queen* (turning to the Negroes) : Farewell and good luck to you. Decent girl that I am, I hope all goes well for you. . . . we've lived a long time; we're now going. . . . we shall lie torpid in the earth like larvae or moles, and if some day . . . ten thousand years hence. . . .[8](p. 126)

But "white" traits such as tenderness and love have to be repressed by the blacks in the same way that "black" traits such as cruelty and hatred have to be repressed by the whites. Neither attempt is wholly successful, for the dialectic between the two remains eternally unresolved—now a partial victory for one, now for the other.

The playwright brings his knowledge of sociological and historical processes and of myth to bear in his exposition of the dialectical forces operating in *The Blacks*—albeit his preference lies with blackness and all it represents: evil, darkness, night, death, play, illusion, femininity, stasis, etc. It seems futile to maintain that Genet has no social concern in *The Blacks*, as some critics do. It cannot possibly have escaped Genet's attention that at the time he wrote the play the former French and English African colonies were emerging as black nations and that at the same time in America the black struggle against a repressive white society was gaining tremendous momentum. It would be equally impossible to say that *The Screens* has nothing at all to do with the Franco-Algerian conflict—a hypothesis exceedingly difficult to square with the historical realities of the time, especially in view of Genet's expressed sympathy with the Algerian rebels. *The Blacks*, therefore, *does* deal, in part, with black revolution, for the characters know exactly what they are doing and possess a goal that may actually prove accessible.

Since the blacks reiterate the theme of revolution persistently, little doubt can remain that Genet intends a certain social concern in the drama—at least as a starting point. In fact, the prophetic quality of the author's social concern in view of contemporary events astounds the audience. In addition to mirroring a developing black revolution, Genet portrays the white society's stubborn refusal to face facts, especially those that are unpleasant. This propensity on the part of the white society becomes ironic when one considers society's preoccupation with "reality" and its reaction against the withdrawal from reality that characterizes dream and play. Society's refusal to face social problems leads to its retreat into ceremony, formality, and etiquette—a retreat parodied in *The Blacks* by the characters' insistence upon ceremony, politeness, and formality. For instance, they wear formal costumes—made to look silly with such incongruous additions as yellow sport shoes for the men. Moreover, they never *tutoyer* each other; that is, they never use the familiar form of address in French with one another. Diouf says to Archibald, "*Je t'en prie* [I beg you]. . . ." And Archibald replies, "Don't use the familiar form with me [*Ne me tutoyez pas*]. Not here. Politeness should be carried to the point where it becomes monstrous" (*Les Nègres*, p. 52).

Ceremony, formality, and etiquette place their practitioners at a distance from each other and insure the kind of alienation that precludes any meaningful relationships. They guarantee that each segment of humanity will never "hear" any of the others. As whites have insulated themselves from the black and his problems, regarding him as the proverbial "invisible man" and never really "hearing" him, so various blacks, on several occasions when white figures interrupt them, resume their speeches after the interruptions end, at the very phrases they were uttering when the interjections occurred. It is as if no intrusions in their thoughts have arisen, as if no whites exist—they are thus figuratively "dead" already for the blacks.

Much more important than his social concern in the play, however, is Genet's interest in archetype and myth and their relationship to the playful ritual that is the drama itself. And in this context, the use of masks takes on significance, for we are all—even the most "civilized" of us—sensitive to the exotic figure of the masked shaman or the disguised dancer. The apparition of the masked figure, as a "purely aesthetic experience, carries us beyond 'ordinary life' into a world where something other than daylight reigns; it carries us back to the world of the savage, the child and the poet, which is the world of play." [9] Using masks, Genet carries us back to the primeval world of myth, a realm in which the matriarchal principle—often considered to precede the patriarchal—dominates *The Blacks* with an insistent imagery. Perhaps the extremely complex figure of the Magna Mater best embodies the matriarchal principle in the drama. We know from artifacts discovered throughout Eurasia and Africa (the Indus Valley, Crete, Turkey, West Africa) that the Mother Cult was almost universal in the mythologies of the prehistoric era. We also know that the Mother assumed many and diverse characteristics and evolved into a multitude of goddesses in various cultures. She was, for instance, the virginal Hellenic Artemis the Huntress and, at the same time, the many-breasted, fertile Artemis of Ephesus. She was Demeter, who caused the grain to grow, and Cybele, who caused her votaries, in fits of madness, to castrate themselves. She was Hera, the nagging wife of Zeus, and Isis, the complaisant, loving wife of Osiris. She was the Babylonian Ishtar, in whose name women gave themselves in love, and the Hindu Kali, in whose name men murdered. Chastity and promiscuity, beneficence and malevolence, love and hate—these were some of the contradictory characteristics that constituted Magna Mater. Genet's portrayal of the matriarchal image includes these and other attributes; indeed, so elaborate is his exploitation of this theme, whether inadvertent or intentional, that he compels us to attend to these issues if we hope register the full address of his meaning.

The evolution of the image of Magna Mater is probably best

traced through Hesiod's *Theogony*, which recapitualtes the process of genesis. First comes the great mother, Earth (Gaea), who gives birth to Sky (Ouranos) parthenogenetically. She couples with her son Sky and produces Kronos (Time) and Rhea, among other children (*Theogony*, II, 116–153). Because of a painful insult delivered to her by her husband, Earth hatches a plan with Kronos, her youngest son, to mutilate Sky. When next Sky comes to couple with his mate, Kronos castrates him with a sickle furnished by Earth, throwing the severed genitals into the ocean (where, some time later, they join with the sea-foam to produce Aphrodite, goddess of love) (*Theogony*, III, 54–210). Now Kronos, the new king, mates with his sister Rhea and produces five children, all of whom he swallows as they are born, for it has been prophesied that he will be overcome by his own son just as he has overcome his father. Rhea, with the help of her mother Earth, saves the sixth child, Zeus, by substituting a rock for the new born baby. Zeus eventually overcomes Kronos, who vomits out all the children—and the rock—he has swallowed. And Zeus proceeds to rule the Universe (*Theogony*, VIII, 453–506). Thus, as Norman O. Brown indicates in the introduction to his translation of Hesiod, female primacy evolves into male primacy from a point where Mother Earth produces children without male partnership to the point where Zeus becomes the ruler of the universe, and he produces Athena parthenogenetically.

Earth, as a symbol of the primeval female, remains forever, but subtler figures like Aphrodite, Athena, Artemis, and Demeter tend to overshadow her as time passes. Aphrodite, for instance, in contrast to Earth, represents the newer female prototype who is sexually dependent upon the male. Her dependence is symbolized by her birth from the severed genitalia of Sky. Her birth "from the father, not the mother, means, in the language of myth . . . subordination to the father."[10] By the same token, Athena's birth signifies male domination of the female. But in a subtle way, even the "dependent" female figures strive to undermine patriarchal order. In Asia Minor, for example, Cybele, in an obvious manifestation of female subversion, causes her male adherents, in fits of frenzy, to castrate themselves and to dress in female clothing thereafter. One is certain that Genet could only approve such rites; castration, of course, is a central feature of *The Balcony*.

Even Aphrodite becomes a symbol of matriarchal reassertion of power as she betrays Hephaistos, her deformed husband, to commit adultery with Ares. Moreover, she has power over all men, even the gods, in matters of sex and love, and often she capriciously uses that power in such a way that the affairs of men are ruined or drastically altered. Demeter, the great Corn-Goddess, presents a symbolic reassertion of the old matriarchal principle against patriarchal sway. When her daughter Persephone (Kore, Proserpine) is abducted by Pluto, Lord of the Dead, no one, not even Zeus, prime symbol of masculine authority, can force the goddess to restore the fertility of the earth until her daughter has been restored to her. When Zeus works out a compromise and Persephone returns to her mother for six-month periods each year, Demeter restores the earth's fertility while her daughter is with her, thus establishing the cycle of the seasons.

But, while we may attempt to analyze some of the facets of Magna Mater, we should bear in mind that our explorations represent only a few twists in a vast labyrinth. Neither the domain of myth nor the domain of Genet's theatre can reduce themselves to simplistic hypotheses. Bearing this in mind, it can be said that Genet in *The Blacks* assigns attributes of the matriarchal archetype primarily to three female characters: Felicity, the Queen, and Virtue. Diouf, who manifests evidence of the matriarchal principle, simultaneously evinces patriarchal characteristics.

Virtue, as depicted by Genet, represents the more sexual aspects of the goddess. She is a black whore who is the only female character in the drama allowed to express even a hint of love. This is because sex and love are integral components of the goddess's nature. Village, by the same token, is the only male character allowed to express love. He is an embodiment of that curious love-hate relationship that exists between the mother and the son-husband. In a revealing speech at the beginning of the play, Archibald, the master of ceremonies, hints at the goddess in Virtue:

> *Village*: I love Virtue. She loves me.
> *Archibald*: Yes, she, perhaps. She has powers that you haven't. . . .
>   She can . . . bring you what most resembles love: tenderness.

In her arms, you'll be her child, not her lover.[11] [Italics mine] (p. 39)

Previous to this speech, Village has expressed a strong hatred for Virtue, implying a symbolic equation between her and Africa, the Great Mother of the blacks:

> *Village:* . . . When I beheld you, suddenly . . . I had the strength to reject everything that wasn't you [her whoredom], and to laugh at the illusion. But my shoulders are very frail. I was unable to bear the weight of the world's condemnation. And I began to hate you when everything about you would have kindled my love and when love would have made men's contempt unbearable, and their contempt would have made my love unbearable. The fact is, I hate you.
>
> . . . .
>
> *Village* (who had lowered his head, raises it to resume his speech): . . . I know not whether you are beautiful. I fear you may be. I fear your sparkling darkness. Oh darkness, stately mother of my race, shadow, sheath that swathes me from top to toe, long sleep in which the frailest of your children would love to be shrouded, I know not whether you are beautiful, but you are Africa, oh monumental night, and I hate you . . . for filling my black eyes with sweetness . . . for making me thrust you from me, for making me hate you. It would take so little for your face, your body, your movements, your heart to thrill me . . .
>
> *Archibald:* Careful, Village!
>
> *Village* (to Virtue): But I hate you![12] (pp. 36–37)

A strong link between Village's venomous, yet tender, attitude and Oedipal love-hate is hard to avoid; Magna Mater always inspires ambivalent feelings in her adherents. Primeval guilt arises out of man's incestuous feeling for his mother, a feeling repressed by the tribal taboo, and, consequently, the love feeling must seek other channels. "With regard to the mother, sensual love becomes *aim-inhibited* and transformed into *affection* (tenderness). Sexuality and affection are divorced; only later are they to meet again in the love for the wife which is sensual as well as tender, aim-inhibited as well as aim-attaining."[13] But there are always traces of the guilt—and the hate that it inspires—attached to the affection felt for the mother.

The Queen represents the "white" (benign) attributes of Magna Mater; she is the Athena-like giver of the arts of civilization:

> *The Judge:* The Queen is asleep. (with a finger to his lips) She's hatching. Hatching what? Celtic remains and the stained-glass windows of Chartres.
>
> *The Governor:* Damn it, wake her up. . . . Give her a dousing, the way they do at the barracks . . .
>
> *The Judge:* You're out of your mind! Who'll do the hatching? You?[14] (p. 43)

However, at this point in the drama, a most interesting development occurs. As the Judge, the Missionary, and the Valet bend over the Queen, trying to waken her, Virtue, directly below the Queen on the stage,[15] suddenly speaks:

> *Virtue* (softly as if in a state of somnambulism [remember that the Queen is still asleep]): I am the lily-white Queen of the West. Only centuries and centuries of breeding could achieve such a miracle! Immaculate, pleasing to the eye and to the soul . . . (The entire Court listens attentively) . . . I am white. If death strikes me, I die in the color of victory. Oh noble pallor, color my temples, my fingers, my belly! Oh eye of mine, delicately shaded iris . . . English lawn, Norman lawn, through you, but what do we see . . .
>
> (The Queen who has finally awakened but is in a dazed state, listens to the poem and then recites along with Virtue)
>
> . . . I am white, it's milk that denotes me, it's the lily, the dove. . . .
>
> . . . .
>
> *Virtue and the Queen* (together): . . . Except that a bit of shade remained in my armpits. . . .[16] (pp. 44-45)

At this point, a subtle change occurs. Virtue by speaking the Queen's words before she herself does, intimates an important equation between herself and the Queen (also symbolized, to some extent, by the sexual unions that Virtue has contracted with whites). The Great Goddess, then, speaks through two voices, and white imperceptibly begins to shade off into black with the allusion to armpits. The transformation is completed shortly thereafter:

> *Virtue* (alone): . . . a swarthy violet, almost black ring is spreading to my cheek. The night. . . .

. . . .
The Queen (suddenly wide awake) That'll do! Silence them,
    they've stolen my voice! Help!...
(Suddenly, Felicity stands up. Everyone looks at her and listens
in silence.)
Felicity: Dahomey!... Dahomey!... Negroes from all corners
    of the earth, to the rescue! Come!... Enter into me, ye multi-
    tudes, and be, for this evening only, my force and reason.[17]

With the intrusion of Felicity, Genet has completed the transformation, and from the lily-white Queen has proceeded through
the white-tainted (but black) Virtue to the completely black
Felicity. Felicity represents the "dark" attributes of the Earth
Mother, who, shrouded in darkness like Demeter, causes the crops
to grow, or like Kali, spawns evil. In one important scene, Felicity
places some grains of corn on the catafalque of the white woman
supposedly dead, murdered by Village:

> (... all turn their heads away. Mrs. Felicity steps down from
> her throne majestically. She goes to the catafalque, bends down
> and slips a few grains under the sheet.)
> *Bobo:* Already!
> *Felicity:* I'm not stuffing her, you know. All the same, it's better
>   for her not to dwindle away.
> *Diouf:* What do you feed her? Rice?
> *Felicity:* Corn [wheat].[18] (p. 50)

By this action, Felicity identifies herself as the Corn Goddess,
giver and taker of the earth's fertility, and thus of life itself:

> [In the ancient world] Corn (wheat) was stored in subterranean
> jars, or *pithoi*, during the barren season. . . . Kore-Persephone's
> residence underground was symbolical of the same corn storage.
> When the jars were opened and the seed brought up, the corn
> maiden ascended to rejoin her mother, the old corn crop. . . .[19]

Felicity is, at the same time, "The Night in person. Not what is
the absence of light, but *the generous and terrible mother who embodies
light and deeds.*"[20] [Italics mine]. In short, she is also the terrible
Mother Kali, who presides over all the illusory ritualistic murders
that take place on and off the stage. And Felicity typifies the

beautiful, but terrifying, power of Kali in one of her speeches toward the end of the play:

> No one could possibly deny it, it's sprouting, sprouting bright and green, it's bursting into bloom, into perfume, and that lovely tree, that crime of mine, is all Africa![21] (p. 102)

The Hindu goddess Kali, perhaps more than all the other personifications of the Great Mother around the world, embodies all her inordinately complex qualities and duties. In Sanskrit, the word for *time* is *kāla*, while *kālā* means "black." Kali, *kāla*, and *kālā* are thus, perhaps, etymologically linked, and the link is confirmed if time is visualized as merciless and black. Those who live under its dominion "are subject to every kind of suffering and to be set free consists primarily in the abolition of time, in an escape from the law of change."[22] The tyrant time can be arrested only in death—or nonbeing—which alone frees. Paradoxically, however, time, in passing, destroys itself; time, therefore, like Mother Kali, signifies both life and death. We pass from the death-like womb of the mother, through life, to the "womb" of Mother Earth, all within the time cycle.

Moreover, an etymological connection can, perhaps, be established between *kāla* and *kālā* on the one hand and *kalā* (art) and *kali* (artifice, play—as in *Kali-yug*, the present age in which man lives, which is an age of deceit and artifice) on the other, for, in the symbolic destruction of the artist's creative impulse while he works on a particular work of art lies the creation of the work of art itself—the whole process occurring within the time cycle, with destruction and creation inseparably linked. Consequently, it is to Kali that artists are often consecrated in India (e. g., *Kali*dasa, author of the famous Sanskrit drama *Shakuntala*), for they are better able to perceive her terrible beauty than ordinary mortals. In her destructive-creative aspect, Kali immediately suggests that most androgynous of all Hindu deities, Shiva, the "Destroyer" of the Hindu trinity. Shiva, also called "The Black One," is often depicted in iconography as the Lord of the Dance. As he dances his dance of destruction, however, he holds one of his hands up in the sign of "Fear not"; in the destruction of his energy lies the creation of the beauty of the dance itself. And he dances within a circle, a geometric figure without a beginning or an end, which symbolizes the everlasting relationship, the eternal dialectic, between evil and good, between destruction and creation. His dance signifies, too, the Hindu cyclical vision of time—a vision shared by Genet.

Kali is often coupled with Shiva in iconography. The pair, indeed, is sometimes represented as a single being, for the goddess is really Shiva's own *shakti*, the female part of his personality, his "power." *Shakti* is also represented as a goddess. She, too, typifies the female aspect of Shiva's personality. As such, she symbolizes the beneficial aspect of the Great Mother principle and, to this extent, is inseparable from the image of Kali. Genet, who has amply expressed his admiration of oriental drama in such documents as his letter to J. J. Pauvert, the avant-garde French publisher,[23] is certain to have included the notion of Kali—consciously or unconsciously—in his theatre.

In the above connection, the audience should not be misled by the scene between Felicity and the Queen at the end of the drama, in which the two are seemingly deadly enemies, for, like all else in *The Blacks*, this too is playful illusion. As a matter of fact, Genet artfully establishes a dialectic between the two women:

> *Felicity:* If you are the light and we the shade, so long as there is night into which day must sink. . . .
> *The Queen:* I'm going to have you exterminated.
> *Felicity* (ironically): You fool, just imagine how flat you'd be without that shade to set you in high relief.[24] (p. 104)

At various times during their debate, the stage directions indicate "The two women advance side by side . . . *in an almost friendly manner*"[25] or "[The Queen] and Felicity start to talk like two women exchanging household recipes."[26] These two seeming opposites must always be contained in each other. One cannot obliterate the other. As was seen in the discussion of Shiva-Kali-Shakti, Magna Mater exemplifies, after all, "Cosmic Power, the totality of the universe, the harmonization of all pairs of opposites, combining wonderfully the terror of absolute destruction with an impersonal yet motherly reassurance. As change, the river of time, the fluidity of life, the goddess at once creates, preserves, and destroys" in an endless cycle.[27]

Genet's cyclical vision of historical time, symbolized by the minuet with which *The Blacks* opens and closes and by the nightly ritual of murder that brings the blacks together to create anew the drama of death and rebirth, causes him to view with objectivity, despite his hatred for the audience, what happens onstage. He knows that the vituperation that he spews upon his white audience is merely the obverse of the love that he might have felt under different circumstances. Consequently, he holds good and evil, white and black in essential balance. Today the effete whites control; the strong blacks serve. Tomorrow the weakening blacks control; the strengthening whites serve. As the Queen intimates in her final speech, the whites will again rise up some day *"dans dix mille ans."*

The realm of myth and archetype so amply illustrated in *The Blacks* shares a common ground with the realm of play, drama, ritual, music, dream, and the dance. The realms are interwoven to such a degree that they are inseparable. In Greece, as is commonly known, tragedy grew out of the ritualized, choreographed "Goat-songs" of an earlier period, sung in honor of Dionysus, the reborn god. And in the classical, religious-oriented drama of both Greece and India, as in primitive cultures, dance and music play indispensible roles. Perhaps one of the best illustrations of the marriage between dance-play and archetype-myth is to be found in the Indian dance-form known as *Kathakali*, in which the participants dance the ancient myths and legends. One should always bear in mind also Shiva (and by extension, Shakti-Kali), whom artists almost invariably represent dancing. Thus, the primeval mind intuitively established the unity between the world of play and myth:

> If in everything that pertains to music we find ourselves within the play-sphere, the same is true in even higher degree of music's twin sister, the dance. Whether we think of the sacred or magical dances of savages, or of the Greek ritual dances, or of the dancing of King David before the Ark of the Covenant, or of the dance simply as part of a festival, it is always at all periods and with all peoples pure play, the purest and most perfect form of play that exists. [28]

In this light, the minuet that opens and closes the ritual of *The Blacks* is of some significance. Mozart's opera *Don Giovanni* furnishes the minuet to which the actors dance, and this too is meaningful. Don Giovanni is an embodiment of the unrepressed, unrepentant, elemental pleasure principle—the dark, erotic force; he signifies the primeval world of the unconscious, of that playfulness of passion that the Christian world equates with evil. To attain his desires, Don Giovanni resorts to the methods of the highly sophisticated, "enlightened," and repressive civilization with which he must deal, a fact symbolized in Mozart's use of the artful, highly structured, organized minuet that accompanies Don Giovanni's seductions. By the same token, the blacks dance the minuet—"play the whites' game"—to attain their ends. And to reinforce the imagery, at the end of the play they gradually switch from the wild rhythms of an African tribal dance to the refined steps of the minuet (see chapt. 4, n. 2) as the curtains close. The switch contains a double meaning. In the first place, it signifies the dark, erotic freedom underlying "blackness," even though blackness must masquerade under "white" attributes. In the second instance, it connotes the ambiguity inherent in the blacks' assumption of power. As they begin to dance the highly organized steps of the minuet after they have won their "victory" over the whites, they symbolically assume, more and more, the effete sophistication of the whites. And so, in a sense, they are betrayed, for in their victory lie the seeds of their defeat.

The theme of betrayal in connection with the figure of Magna Mater is probably best illustrated in the extremely enigmatic figure of Diouf. Diouf, the male who masquerades as a woman— the Man-Woman, so to speak—suggests those primeval androgynous gods one finds in primitive cultures as well as in India. Significantly, it is Felicity who "gives birth" to Diouf's masquerade, for it is she who orders him to assume the role of the White Woman about to be raped and murdered by Village. And it is Felicity who plays the White Woman's mother during the masquerade. But she has prepared the audience for her role already by placing corn on the catafalque, thus associating herself with Demeter, the grain goddess. Diouf thus recalls those priests of Cybele, the Great

Mother of Phrygia and also one of the aspects of Demeter, who became "women" before they could enter her service.

When Diouf assumes his role as the White Woman, Virtue seals the ceremony with a blasphemous chant. Just as the solemn *Hoc est corpus* of the Roman Catholic Communion service becomes perverted by the popular tongue into the magical formula "hocus-pocus," so Virtue takes the Roman Catholic litanies of the Blessed Virgin Mary and transforms them into an obscene parody, the "Litanie des Blêmes." Diouf and Village, thereupon, proceed with the ritual reenactment of Village's "crime" step by step. Diouf now gives symbolic birth to five white puppets, representing the five Great Figures on the stage. And the "birth" occurs before a white member of the audience, who has previously been summoned to the stage to hold the White Woman's knitting. He is there as the audience's surrogate exactly to witness this "birth," which makes Diouf the symbolic mother of the white race. Village, representative of the blacks, then rapes, strangles, and disembowels the symbolic White Mother.

One of the clues to Genet's murder-ritual lies, one is sure, in Diouf's subsequent resurrection and elevation to the white "heaven" where the Great White Figures are located. Diouf's "murder" is, to be sure, a foreshadowing of the assassination of the Queen and her entourage. The "murder" of Diouf symbolizes the blacks' desire to eradicate the "white" aspects of the Great Mother. The ressurrection of Diouf proves the impossibility of such a task. Though the "white" features of Magna Mater may remain submerged for a time like Persephone, they must eventually reappear, for they must remain a part of the Mother's image. The Queen, too, intimates her own resurrection in her last speech in the play. Genet, it seems, offers the sacrificial rite to prove the eternal aspect of the Earth Mother image in all her facets.

But the problematical Diouf becomes important as a patriarchal as well as a matriarchal image. In the final analysis, after all, Diouf is a fatherly black, somewhat at odds with Felicity and the younger blacks concerning procedures to be followed in dealing with the whites. He is not a white woman at all, but rather the paternal voice of order and reason, counseling moderation. If Felicity incarnates black motherhood, then Diouf incarnates black fatherhood. This view is supported by Diouf's role when, masked as a white, he assumes the paternalistic attitude of the whites toward the blacks—an attitude abhorred by the blacks. He embodies doubly, therefore, the father image. He even evinces patriarchal pregnancy envy, for, in the ancient myth cycles, the male, in assuming the primacy previously held by the female, invariably longs also to inherit her fertility; he envies her ability to bear children and attempts to arrogate the function of pregnancy for himself. This attempt illustrates the desire to become androgynous and, consequently, totally free from dependence upon the female for procreative purposes (and thus also free of the genital organization of society—a freedom symbolized by the castration scene in *The Balcony*). Aphrodite's birth from Ouranos's genitalia, Kronos's swallowing of his infants as they are born— these acts manifest the male's pregnancy envy. But it is a desire doomed never to be truly fulfilled, a fact symbolized by Kronos's ingestion of a barren rock instead of his sixth child and his subsequent regurgitation of all the ingested children after his defeat by Zeus, a defeat caused by the trickery of Earth. So, even in her defeat, the image of Magna Mater, in typical Genet fashion, plays the game of "loser wins," for she wins at least a partial victory over her eternal adversary, the dominant male principle. And so it is with Diouf, too, for his act of giving birth to five puppets is as sterile as Kronos's attempts at pregnancy.

The ritual murder of Diouf, then, provides us once again with the spectacle of Zeus defeating Kronos. And Kronos, it must be remembered, was defeated at the behest of his wife Rhea with the help of Earth, both Great Mother figures. In the play, it is Felicity, the Black Mother, who chooses Diouf, the Black Father, as sacrificial subject, and who orders one of her "sons," Village, to perform the sacrifice.

But Diouf is resurrected and elevated to the "upper" world to oversee the world of the blacks. The patriarch

> guarantees the biological and sociological basis on which the history of mankind depends. The annihilation of his person threatens to annihilate lasting group life itself and to restore the prehistoric and subhistoric destructive force of the pleasure principle. But the sons want the same thing as the father; they

want lasting satisfaction of their needs. They can attain this objective only by repeating, *in a new form*, the order of domination which had controlled pleasure and thereby preserved the group. *The father survives as the god.*[29] [Italics mine]

We know of Genet's cyclical vision of history, and he intimates strongly in the play that the blacks will repeat "in a new form" that which the whites have done. The figure of Magna Mater now begins to take on added significance, for she becomes one of Genet's beloved outlaws. By operating surreptitiously to subvert the father's authority—that is, established, rational order—the Great Mother attains the greatest saintliness in Genet's scheme. She is good and she is evil; she is black and she is white; she is life and she is death. Like his own natural mother, the whore who abandoned him unnaturally to the care of the state, she is the eternal matriarchal outlaw, symbol of the primeval and chaotic unconscious, attempting to betray patriarchal order—and thus establishing the compelling dialectic that is, for Genet, at the heart of the cosmos.

5 | THE SCREENS

After *The Blacks*, Genet turned his artistic talents to a play based on the Franco-Algerian conflict of the early sixties. The result was the most disparate and, in many ways, the most incomprehensible of his dramas, *The Screens* (*Les Paravents*). He himself wrote the following to Roger Blin, the brilliant Parisian director who staged most of his dramas, in a letter concerning Blin's production of *The Screens:*

> People say that plays are generally supposed to have a meaning: not this one. It's a celebration whose elements are disparate, it is a celebration of nothing. [1]

We have the author's own word, therefore, that, although the play may not have any "meaning" in the usual sense, its theme is *nothingness*. The passage quoted above is perhaps another way for Genet to say that he had completed his creative work in the dramatic medium in the way most acceptable to him—that is, by the attainment of nothingness, for the conclusion of this final drama centers on absolute nothingness, Genet's metaphor for perfection, as all characters and things desert the stage to leave it completely empty and dark:

> During the last two or three speeches, the dead carried off their screens. The Mother leaves last, with her armchair. *The stage is empty. It's all over.* [2] [Italics mine] (p. 201)

In this play, then, Genet attains what, for him, is perfection. It does not say anything new; it recapitulates his *oeuvre*. As a matter of fact, the one most evident feature of *The Screens* is that Genet says nothing really new. All of his previous statements about play, myth, ritual, and illusion are reiterated forcefully—if ambiguously. Thus, the drama becomes a kind of complete summation of his previous dramatic works. Since many years have passed since he wrote the play, it is reasonably safe to assume that Genet has no further intention of working in the area of drama as a means of artistic expression. He has presented in *The Screens* his ultimate and negative "Ave atque vale"—at least in the theatre. Any dramatic piece he writes hereafter would seem to be anticlimactic unless he strikes out into new thematic areas. One feels that the only remaining aesthetic area open to his artistic exploration and his genius is the cinema, a proposition to be discussed at more length in the appendix.

Since Genet summarizes his *oeuvre* in *The Screens*, it is of value to note exactly *what* he does and *how* he does it. I should, however, in passing, note my agreement with the judgment of Josephine Jacobsen and William R. Mueller in regard to the drama:

> [*The Screens*] to some extent bogs down in its own theatricality. It becomes at too many points an accumulation of *things*, of props, so that the actors and the characters they portray tend to disappear into the tiers, drawings, screens, offstage sounds, floating objects and the like. [3]

It may be that this is exactly Genet's intent—to cause even the actors in the theatre to become an abstraction, and ultimately an Absence; an intent somewhat enhanced by the confusing multiplicity of roles played by a relatively small number of actors, so that the audience is rendered incapable of following any but a few main characters. But, if such is the case, the author fails, for the main characters etch themselves too strongly on the minds of the spectators (Saïd, Leïla, Warda) to indicate abstraction.

As for the technique that Genet uses to achieve his purpose, it becomes one of the paramount features of the drama. In *The Balcony*, the use that the author made of moveable screens to enhance the sense of ambiguity surrounding that shady domain where illusion and reality combine was noted. In *The Blacks* was seen the author's utilization of different physical levels of the stage (his positioning of the White Personages on a platform elevated above the floor of the stage, where the blacks performed) to symbolize the "superiority" of whites. In *The Screens*, Genet exploits both the moveable screens of the former play and the various physical levels of the stage of the latter to reinforce the metaphysical imagery surrounding the indistinct outlines of illusion and reality and their concomitants, death and life, play and work, unconscious and conscious. Genet desires that the director of this play use screens so big that no ordinary theatrical stage could contain them; he should, instead, present the spectacle out-of-doors:[4]

> This is how this play should be staged: In an open-air theater. A rectangular area enclosed within a high board fence. The back and the sides of the stage are to be formed by high, uneven boards, painted black. They are to be arrayed in such a way that platforms of different heights can be brought onstage from the left and right. There will thus be an extremely varied set of stages, levels, and surfaces. The screens and actors will enter and leave through spaces between the boards, right and left.[5] (p. 9)

The Screens thus becomes the most completely Artaudian spectacle that Genet—or any other contemporary theatrical writer—has produced, for he evokes his metaphysical images not only through the grand sweep of spectacle, but also through excessive use of mask and/or make-up[6] and through his complete immersion of the audience in cruelty, filth, and degradation. As in *The Blacks*, the point of departure for *The Screens* lies in Genet's social concern, for the drama occurs during the Algerian struggle for independence from the French. Saïd, an Arab youth, accompanied by his mother (called simply "La Mère" in the play), is on his way to wed Leïla, a girl so ugly that she never removes the black hood that covers her face throughout the spectacle. After the marriage, as the Algerian rebellion gains momentum, Saïd is propelled through a series of incarcerations for thefts he has perpetrated against coworkers and colleagues. Leïla, too, goes to prison for theft. The mother, after her rejection by her peers and her desertion by her son and her daughter-in-law, dies and subsequently reappears in the region of the dead, where she discovers Kadidja, one of those who had rejected her, and a number of other characters who have died. Thereafter,

Leïla dies, and Saïd, after betraying the Algerian rebel cause, is executed. Neither ever appears in the region of the dead.

A subplot—if one can speak of plot at all in *The Screens*—concerns Warda and Malika, two prostitutes. Warda, the older of the two by about twenty years, is proud of her whoredom and always attempts to project its eloquent imagery through her mode of dress. When, however, whoredom loses its air of mystery and glamour because of the progress of the revolution, Warda rips her dress to shreds and wears rags until she dies at the hands of the jealous village wives shortly thereafter. After her death, Warda, too, enters the land of the dead.

The dramatic techniques used to present all these events in *The Screens* suggest playfulness on the part of the author; indeed, even the characters themselves indulge in pretense and play-acting. For instance, Genet uses the aforementioned screens in such a way that they become not only sets, but also symbolic drawing boards on which various characters draw objects from time to time. Moreover, each actor must play five or six roles in the play, the sex indicated for these roles being of no importance; males may play female roles, and vice-versa. Thus, Genet attempts to convey the feeling that, as in all his other theatre, impersonation and play are at the heart of the drama—an impression reinforced by his directions concerning make-up:

> The Characters
>
> If possible, they will be masked. If not, highly made up, heavily disguised (even the soldiers). Excessive make-up, contrasting with the realism of the costumes. It is best to provide a large variety of false noses. . . . No face should retain the conventional beauty of feature which is played up all too often on both stage and screen. [7] (p. 10)

And Genet does not stipulate that Arabs play the roles of Arabs—a departure from *The Blacks*, in which the actors playing the roles of blacks *must*, according to Genet, be black themselves. [8] Apparently, the author intends a further reinforcement of the aura of play-acting and impersonation. Or perhaps there is a much simpler explanation: any actor may play an Arab's role because an Arab is, after all, racially "white." The latter explanation would tend to make the French colonialists' patronizing judgments of the Arabs even more grotesque than they seem at first sight in the drama.

A further heightening of the motifs of play and illusion occurs in the use of real objects in juxtaposition with the unreal:

> One or more real objects must always be on the stage, in contrast with the objects drawn in *trompe-l'oeil* on each screen.[9] (p. 9)

Furthermore, actors must, at various times, draw objects or actions on the screens, or they must make sounds indicating the presence of animals or the occurrence of natural phenomena. For example, at one juncture, while two of the French *colons* converse, Arabs appear onstage to draw yellow flames around the orange trees depicted symbolically on the screens. On numerous other occasions, either the Mother or Leïla imitates the sounds of animals supposedly nearby. Play and its correlatives—play-acting, impersonation, illusion, dream, ritual, myth, and negation —then, all appear in *The Screens* to sum up forcefully what Genet has signified about play already in his earlier dramas.

Play-acting, impersonation, and illusion must occupy a central position in any discussion of this drama as in any of his others. As in *The Maids*, in which maids impersonate their mistress; as in *The Balcony*, in which characters impersonate other characters whose roles they envy; or as in *The Blacks*, in which black cooks, deacons, and medical students act out different roles on the stage each night; so in *The Screens*, actors imitate animals or natural sounds, or, like Blankensee, they enhance illusions about themselves by making themselves appear more substantial through the use of padding on the stomach and the backside. And just as the bordello patrons in *The Balcony* are excessively made up or just as blacks wear masks in *The Blacks*, so characters in *The Screens* either don masks or wear heavy make-up. The uses to which Genet puts impersonation and illusion in his theatre are, of course, manifold. In the first place, he establishes an artful dialectic between reality and illusion and, by extension, between good and evil. As a matter of fact, much of the action in his dramas occurs in the twilight world between illusion and reality, where confusion between the two worlds confounds the spectator. In *The Screens*, Genet presents this confusion repeatedly in his insistence that one *real* object always be onstage. When the play opens, for example, a pile of rocks and a milestone are onstage. On the other hand, in one scene, Leïla reproduces a clock (which she has stolen) as a drawing on one of the screens when it would be far easier to employ a real clock. And, at the same time, she produces a cheese grater, a lamp, and a glass—real items that she has stolen—from beneath her skirt. But the clock reproduced on the screen commands the audience's attention, for it is far more fanciful than any prosaic, real clock could be, and it is important that the clock, of all the stolen items, be represented as an illusion, a drawing. Clocks, the measuring sticks of *time*, have no place in the realm of illusion, play, and dream, where time and space are irrelevant concepts, for this realm stands apart from time—it is *timeless*. Moreover, the "realistic" space-time continuum is completely disoriented in those scenes involving the dead and the living. In some scenes, the dead characters are located on the lowest level of the stage, looking *down* on the actions of the living, which occur *above* them on the stage. In other scenes, they are *above* the living and look *up* at the actions taking place below them. Space, then, like time, is outside the sphere of illusion, dream, and play.

The second important use to which Genet puts impersonation and illusion is the intensification of mythic and archetypal imagery. In this context, various figures become important. Warda, Kadidja, the Mother, and Ommou, for instance, are primeval mother figures, symbolic of the same eternal maternal outlaw presented in *The Blacks*, who attempts to subvert patriarchal order and who, by her subversion, establishes the necessary tension between order and chaos, reason and unreason, reality and fantasy. The attachment of these figures to Saïd augments the imagery of matriarchal traitor as I shall show later. The archetypal Colonialist, on the other hand, represents the primeval father; he enhances his commanding presence by padding himself fore and aft or by leaving his glove behind him in the air as a presence to command the servile Arab employees. Like the primeval father, the French *colon* commands the obedience and the hatred of his subordinate sonlike Algerian workers:

> *Sir Harold* (irritated): . . . Am I no longer the boss?
> *Malik:* Oh yes, of course you are, Sir Harold. You're our father.
> Too bad we're not your children.[10] (p. 70)

And like the primeval father, the *colon* is deprived of his power by his "sons." The Arabs discover first that Sir Harold's glove, the symbol of his presence that remains to watch over them even when Sir Harold is absent, is really stuffed with straw. And they proceed then, in secret, to burn his orange groves, which represent his power. Moreover, they kill Monsieur Blankensee shortly after an Arab maid discovers the substantial padding that he uses on his stomach and his buttocks, a padding representing the power he displays. Significantly, the last time we see the *colons* in the final scene, they are all in rags, having lost all their power. And Warda, too, when she loses her power, rips her dress into rags.

Unlike the *colons*, the commanding female figures in the drama seem to augment their power to a certain degree as the play progresses. It is at the instigation of primordial mother figures such as Kadidja and Ommou, for instance, that the Arabs' revolution against the French commences and intensifies. And the Arabs, until close to the end of the drama, listen to and obey these female figures. But as the revolution succeeds, it takes on more and more of the aspects of the hated French regime, much to the dismay of the female figures, both dead and alive. As in *The Blacks* and *The Balcony*, the success of the revolution is the beginning of its failure. In *The Balcony*, the reality-oriented revolution fails when it succumbs to illusion; that is, when it accepts the mock figures as authentic representatives of the supposedly fallen regime. And in *The Blacks*, the blacks begin to assume "whiteness" as they dance the minuet, a white dance, after their defeat of the whites. So in *The Screens*, the Arabs become more European as they begin to conquer. The Arabs, like the primeval sons, repeat the old patriarchal order once they have eliminated the repressive father-like French. In this context, Warda takes on importance. She symbolizes the erotic energy of the Great Mother, an energy shrouded in mystery and made the

more appealing by its mystery. She is proud of the fact that Arab
prostitutes, unlike the French prostitutes, do not undress for
their clients. It is the men who undress like whores in order to
enter the prostitutes, who remain dressed, the better to maintain and project their erotic power and mystery:

> *Warda:* ... When the sun's gone down, I can't do a thing
> without my finery ... not even spread my legs to piss, but
> rigged up in gold I'm the Queen of Showers.[11] (p. 18)

And again:

> *Malika:* Not just anyone can approach our thighs. One has to
> knock before entering.
> *Warda* (haughtily, same drawling, disillusioned voice): Twenty-
> four years! ... A whore's not something you can improvise.
> She has to ripen. It took me twenty-four years. And I'm gifted!
> A man, what's that? A man remains a man. In our presence, it's
> he who strips like a whore from Cherbourg or Le Havre.[12]
> (p. 19)

But the mystery and the power surrounding and enhancing
erotic energy erodes as the Algerians begin to turn the tide in
favor of victory against the French. The Arab soldiers come to
the bordello now, in completely unabashed and straightforward,
businesslike fashion, to fornicate and merely to fornicate, not to
admire Warda's image and bask pleasantly in her mystery and
her power. At this point, Warda rips to shreds her costume,
symbol of the power of her enshrouded eroticism, because of her
realization that she and her profession have become mere ad-
juncts of the reality principle. The whores exist now only as a
brief, pleasant respite from the tedious real world of the revolution. They are treated like toys, to be paid for and used occasion-
ally and then to be put aside and forgotten so that patrons can
enter the reality-dominated world outside. Gone are the days
when clients basked in the harlot's mystery and carried its image
with them after they had left her presence:

> *Warda:* Mirror, mirror, where is the time when I could stare at
> myself, and yawn, for hours on end? (She spits on the mirror.)
> Where are the men who used to stare at me staring at myself

without daring to breathe? Now we plug away. And answering hello to the women who greet you at the grocer's is less restful than I'd have thought. . . .

. . . .

[Once] . . . there was a Sahara Desert between me, Warda, and the most despised woman of the village, between me and Leïla. A major in the Colonial Artillery—I'm speaking of a year ago—turned up one afternoon, three of his buttons were loose: it was he, with his fat ringed fingers, who sewed them on his fly, I didn't know how to. Now I do. Suck the thread, thread the needle. . . . At the butcher's, at the grocer's, they say hello to me. . . . I'm less and less someone. . . . And my anger is greater and greater and so is my sadness. [13] (p. 139)

Shortly afterwards, Djemila arrives at the brothel—Djemila, the Algerian prostitute from France, who brings with her the French fashion of undressing for the patrons and whom the rebels will now prefer to Warda. Djemila has learned, like the European whore, that sex can be a commodity to be sold on the open market. It is stripped of all the ritual, of all the power, and of all the mystery that Warda represents. Subsequent to Djemila's arrival, Warda dies, for she finds herself in an untenable situation in which her image has been shattered and in which her sexuality, her power, and her mystery have been shackled by the reality principle.

Sexuality, once a pleasurable mystery, has become open, businesslike, and uninhibited, but in losing its mystery it also loses its pleasure and its sense of liberation from the everyday world:

> . . . one can speak of "repressive de-sublimation": release of sexuality in modes and forms which reduce and weaken erotic energy. In this process too, sexuality spreads into formerly tabooed dimensions and relations. However, instead of re-creating these dimensions and relations in the images of the Pleasure Principle, the opposite tendency asserts itself: the Reality Principle extends its hold over Eros. The most telling illustration is provided by the methodical introduction of sexiness into business, politics, propaganda, etc. *To the degree to which sexuality obtains a definite sales value or becomes a token of prestige and of playing according to the rules of the game, it is itself transformed into an instrument of social co-*

> *hesion. Emphasis of this familiar trend may illuminate the depth of the gap which separates even the possibilities of liberation from the established state of affairs.* [14] [Italics mine]

In the final analysis then, the treacherous female figures are themselves betrayed when the victorious Algerians adopt the modes of the French, including their sexual behavior with prostitutes, their rationality, and their social cohesion:

> *Ommou* (to The [Algerian] Combatant): We have nothing to do with you. *You reason.*
> *The Combatant: If you want to organize, you've got to reason.* What are we combatants entitled to?
>
> . . . .
> *Before long, we'll all be reasoners. . . .* [15] [Italics mine] (p. 194)

Reason and order begin to assert themselves in the hitherto disordered, disparate Arab guerilla army, and, as they do, the matriarchal domain of the irrational is betrayed into submission to and domination by its eternal adversary. Since the betraying females are themselves betrayed, they bless Saïd, the archtraitor, throughout the drama, for he is uncompromisingly the traitor from beginning to end. It is he who maintains the balance between the realms of being and nothingness, reality and illusion, in his choice of those traits opposed to the traits normally accepted by the society surrounding him.

Saïd (along with Leïla) becomes an image of the loathsome, filthy, undesired Other—the fearsome Other that is Unconscious, Dream, and Play. That Other, repressed in the work-oriented world of the reality principle and considered as Evil, reasserts itself in Saïd to such a great extent that the audience must face it. And the image becomes not only hateful, but grossly excremental. Excrement as a symbol for the Other and its connection with criminality and betrayal become artfully manipulated by Genet to exalt the play impulse in man, for the child knows intuitively that life is of the body, and, no matter how much "the repressed and sublimating adult may consciously deny it, the fact remains that life is of the body and only life creates values." [16]

For the child, excrement, as a product of his own body, is an object of narcissistic love with which he fondly plays. It is only later that he learns from adults that his excrement is hateful, and he learns to associate this loathing with his body, which produces the awful product. At this point, "infantile sexuality come to its catastrophic end, non-bodily cultural objects inherit the symbolism originally attached to the anal product, but only as second-best substitutes for the original (sublimation)."[17] Genet reasserts excrementalism in Saïd and Leïla to intensify its primacy in the life of the body and to point out the folly of man's repression and abhorrence of it, for the excremental expresses a longing for the childlike play impulse. In rejecting the excremental, man opts for repression instead of liberation.

Criminality and betrayal go hand in hand with excrementalism in *The Screens*. And when these traits appear in Saïd and Leïla, they strengthen Genet's attempt to force his audience to come to terms with the Other, which is, after all, an important component of the Self. The Other is that which is repressed in the Self, for it is that which is considered evil and, therefore, not truly of the Self by the common run of men. We must remember, however, that it is only Saïd and Leïla, those representatives of the Other, who, at the end of the drama, have attained complete liberation; they never appear in the land of the dead, although the dead await them with great anticipation:

> *The Mother* (anxiously): What about Saïd? Is he coming?
> . . . .
> *The Mother:* Saïd! . . . I'll simply have to wait for him. . . .
> Kadidja (laughing): Don't bother. He'll no more be back than will Leïla.[18] (p.201)

Saïd and Leïla consciously choose criminality; Saïd betrays the Algerian cause; they both die under sordid conditions; and they both attain complete liberation, unlike the souls of the other dead, which are imprisoned in a sort of Hades. These souls are imprisoned until they too can achieve the liberation that is escape into—or, better, acceptance of—total nonbeing. Moreover, neither Saïd nor Leïla repent their guilt for their crimes; rather, they exult in their crimes and their guilt. If we consider how someone acquires a sense of guilt, we come to the indisputable conclusion that a person feels guilt when he has done something

86

bad or *sinful*. In some cases, he need not even have committed the
offensive act, but just *considered* it, in order to feel guilty. However, what is "bad" is often not at all what is injurious to the ego;
it might even be enjoyable. Yet one still feels guilt. Freud declares
that this feeling of guilt stems from the child's fear of the loss of
love of a parent:

> If he loses the love of another person on whom he is dependent,
> he also ceases to be protected from a variety of dangers. Above
> all, he is exposed to the danger that this stronger person will
> show his superiority in the form of punishment. . . . *therefore,
> what is bad is whatever causes one to be threatened with loss of love.
> For fear of that loss, one must avoid it.*[19] [Italics mine]

In this light, Saïd's choice of evil is very important. He shuns
love; he will not allow himself that luxury for fear of losing his
freedom of option. And he is contemptuous of any punishment
he may receive for his actions. He says shortly before his execution—an execution that he contemptuously accepts—"To the
old lady, to the soldiers, to all of you, I say shit." At this point,
he is like Lefranc in *Deathwatch*, like Solange and Claire in *The
Maids*, like the Chief of Police in *The Balcony* in his complete
isolation—he is "really alone," in the words of Lefranc. But,
again like the characters in the other three plays, he accomplishes
his liberation through his deliberate isolation of himself from
the world. When his conscious and pleasurable choice of criminality, of evil, and of betrayal occurs, his total liberation from the
repressive strictures of a reality-oriented society occurs. This
complete liberation is symbolized in his nonappearance at the
end of the play. He has become the all-pervasive and silent Absence represented by the stage directions at the final curtain, the
Absence that is, for Genet, perfection.

CONCLUSION

At the end of any study of Genet, the critic finds himself emotionally and intellectually exhausted because, unsuspecting, he has allowed the author to seduce him intellectually, to lure him, caught in the enveloping net of Genet's fantasy, to the brink of the abyss of Self. And if the preceding chapters have done nothing else, they have shown that the viewer (or the reader) becomes enmeshed in the dazzling web which Genet constructs for him. "Touch the visible leaves of any recent Genet play," writes Joseph McMahon, "and you are bound to find yourself pulling at tough, resistant roots—into the depths of yourself." [1] To illuminate the depths of that Self, Genet uses the play element repeatedly in his drama. For instance, he playfully manipulates man's concepts of ritual, myth, and illusion to immerse the audience in evil so that it is forced to face the repressed Other in the Self—and to face it as a valid, though unknowable, component of the Self. This unknowable component of Self might be called the *unconscious*. It is the realm of dream, of play, of illusion, of negation, of pleasure—the realm that in the real world of the everyday occurrence is suspect because of its intangibility and its incomprehensibility. It is, by extension, the domain of evil too, for instinct has free and unrepressed sway there. And since the unconscious is considered evil, it is believed to be Other than Self; it is, consequently, repressed whenever possible and subordinated to the comprehensible rational world.

It is Genet's purpose, in part, to reassert and reaffirm this Other within the Self. To that end, he has become a dedicated irrationalist in a society still perversely clinging to eighteenth-century rationalism, and in that sense he is a romantic. Of course, he does not stand alone in his awareness of Self and Other as an entity. Certainly the ancient Taoists had this same awareness, as did the seventeenth-century metaphysical poets in England and as do such modern theorists as Nietzsche, Freud, and Jung. For example, such Jungian concepts as the *anima*, or the "female" in every man, and the *animus*, or the "male" in every woman, bespeak this awareness eloquently. What sets Genet apart, however, is his absolute insistence upon that Other, the better to assert its claim to legitimacy, or, perhaps, the better to assert its right to *illegitimacy*. Illustrative of this point is Lefranc in *Deathwatch*, who achieves Otherness when he becomes an outcast in both the criminal and "straight" worlds. He achieves his ends through losing his contest of criminality with Green Eyes. Lefranc has *consciously willed* an act that should have sprung unbidden from the primordial region of the unconscious, i.e., his strangulation of Maurice. But, paradoxically, by losing he wins, for in willing the murder he unites rationality and irrationality—reality and fantasy—into a whole. It is for this reason that he is completely isolated at the end of the drama, for it is no mean feat to attain this synthesis of the two worlds; few, if any, ever achieve it. And Lefranc intuits his position at the end of the play in his cry of exultant despair that he is *really* alone.

Similarly, the maids in *The Maids* are able to unite reality and illusion in their daily games of impersonation. And if, as Genet would have it, the director of *The Maids* employs adolescent boys to play the parts of Claire and Solange, the imagery of synthesis becomes even more forceful. Genet further desires that a poster exposing the fact that boys are assuming women's roles be posted in a dominant place on or near the stage. And thus the imagery expands almost endlessly; boys play at being women, who in turn play at being their mistress. In this context, Genet's thoughts on Tiresias, the blind seer of ancient Thebes, become important:

> This may not be an original thought with me, but let me restate it anyway, that the patron saint of actors is Tiresias,

because of his dual nature. Legend has it that he retained the male
sex for seven years, and for seven more, the other. For seven
years a man's clothing, for seven a woman's. In a certain way,
at certain moments—or perhaps always—his femininity followed in close pursuit of his virility, the one or the other being
constantly asserted, with the result that he never had any rest, I
mean any specific place where he could rest. Like him, the
actors are neither this nor that, and *they must be aware that they
are a presence constantly beset by femininity or its opposite,* but ready
to play to the point of abasement that which, be it virility or
its opposite, is in any case predetermined.

Saint Tiresias, the patron saint of actors.

As for divinatory powers of the saint, let every actor make
an effort *to see clearly* within himself.[2] [Italics mine]

In *The Maids,* male and female become united in the boy
actors as reality and illusion become united in the impersonations
of the maids. In the games of the maids the imagination achieves
equality with the reality principle, and in the ultimate game at
the end of the drama the maids achieve the same kind of liberating
isolation that Lefranc attains in *Deathwatch* as they *will* Claire's
murder-suicide during her final impersonation of Madame at
the curtain.

Of course, the Chief of Police in *The Balcony* exemplifies the
cohesion of Self and Other too as he attains his apotheosis at the
end of the drama, an apotheosis achieved primarily through
the self-castration of his alter ego, Roger. This castration asserts
the androgynous principle through a rejection of our genitally
oriented society and an affirmation of the sexually undifferentiated
period of early childhood. Just as the ancient priests of Cybele
"united" male and female in themselves through their acts of
self-mutilation, so does the image of the Chief of Police. The
priests, after their castration, donned women's clothes, the better
to reinforce the "female" in themselves, to put it on an equal
footing with the "male." By the same token, they might be
considered the living dead, evincing all of life's functions except
those of reproduction; that is, those that insure the perpetuation
of life. They stood, in other words, on that same tenuous ground
between illusion and reality, between life and death, between

male and female, on which the Chief of Police stands. His castration, too, acknowledges the union of woman and man in himself. It also avows the oneness of life and death when the Chief descends into a tomb to perpetuate his image into immortality.

In *The Blacks*, it is the Great Mother figures, like Felicity, the Queen, and Virtue who exemplify, in the words of Joseph Campbell, "the totality of the universe, the harmonization of all pairs of opposites." [3] They evince, perhaps, more evil than good, more black than white, more death than life, but they do so merely to imprint forcefully in the viewer's imagination those irrational attributes that, in the real world outside the theatre, he would foolishly deny.

The spectacular, disparate *The Screens* reiterates again, in many ways, Genet's notion of the unity of opposites such as Self and Other, life and death, reality and illusion. For instance, Genet writes to Blin concerning the dead in the drama:

> I see the dead as being heavily made-up—but with green the dominant color. White clothing, suggestive of winding sheets. Their diction will be different. *It will be louder and closer to everyday language.* [4] [Italics mine]

The dead are heavily made up in the color of growing things and of life, green; and their speech is closer to lively everyday speech than that of the living, whose speech is sometimes grandiloquent and stately.

The major character around whom the drama revolves, Saïd, is an isolated man from the opening curtain. He has not to aspire to his splendid isolation as did Lefranc and the Chief of Police; he has already achieved it. And he progresses from this isolated state to total abstraction and absence at the end of the drama, for "an extraordinary emptiness has more presence than the most dense fullness," [5] says Genet. Saïd asserts Other more uncompromisingly than any other dramatic character created by the author. He does so for a variety of reasons. In the first place, since the play appears to be the last drama Genet will write, he wanted Saïd to enunciate Other as forcefully and as convincingly as possible to reestablish its position of equality with Self. In the second place, Saïd seems to be spokesman for Genet himself, who has now become a respectable artist in the eyes of a detested bourgeois society. In this light, Saïd may be said to be the ultimate denial by the author of that society, with its accent on the good, the real, and the beautiful. Like Saïd, Genet refuses to become one of society's adornments; he chooses instead to become one of its afflictions. He wills himself to be one of society's "losers." He refuses to play its game; he insists on inventing his own game. As in his homosexuality, his criminality, and his treachery, he plays the game of "loser wins" in dramas that redefine the eternal dialectic between good and evil. If his dramas suggest the imminent victory of the dark, repressed forces of the irrational, the unconscious, and the imagination over the regimented, repressive forces of the rational, the conscious, and the reality principle, it is only to impress the validity of that eternal dialectic forcefully upon the Western audience. And, above all, these dramas are designed to reveal to mankind how trivial are its notions of diabolism, how diabolic are its passions, how sacred to the character of the Self is its passion for the profane, how profane are the customs, morals, laws of modern civilization. It would be inaccurate to say that our civilization totally ignores this obsessive matter. But it is perhaps true to say that Genet has recast Western obsessions into forms of his own strange contrivance—ritual play-forms in which the profane is liberated, the sacred is redefined, and both are given a new equilibrium.

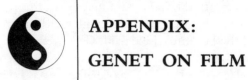

APPENDIX:
GENET ON FILM

The contrast between Genet's theatrical *oeuvre* and his only film,[1] *Chant d'amour (Love Song)*,[2] is an engaging one. By the time that Genet began to work in the dramatic form, he was a literary craftsman, having perfected his writing art in the novels. However, when he made his film—one is tempted to say his *first* film in the hope that there will be others—he struck out into a completely new artistic field, one in which the medium is graphic rather than literary. In *Chant d'amour*, the rather self-conscious amateurishness of the director making his first film often replaces the consummate skill of the mature literary artist. Nevertheless, there are enough artistically beautiful moments in the film to warrant the knowledgeable viewer's anticipation of a second Genet film at some point in the future. Because the film has been banned in the few places in the world where it has been shown publicly, the interested critic must resort to the literary underground in order to see it, which is unfortunate because, despite its unabashed presentation of some explicitly pornographic material, it remains a poetic document of an important artist's world view.

All the themes that preoccupied the early Genet—homosexuality, masturbation, fantasy—are in the film. Made in 1950, if the viewer is to believe the inscription at the end of the film, it reflects a still developing Genet's preoccupations with the connection between playful fantasy on the one hand and reality on the other and with the twilight world between the two. In truth, it would seem that film itself, which is probably the very best contemporary medium for projecting the world of illusion,

92

must, by its very nature, appeal to Genet as the most congenial vehicle for his artistic themes.

Since few people have seen the film, it is probably wise to furnish a detailed summary of it. One of the most important features of the film is the fact that it does away with words entirely, for it is silent, relying solely on visual images to convey the drama. It opens with a view of an immense brick wall, which turns out to be the wall surrounding a prison. The camera slowly pans the outside of the prison itself and homes in on two adjoining cell windows, one with a hand dangling from it, clutching a garland of flowers and swinging it toward the other window, from which another hand protrudes, trying to catch the garland. The camera cuts to a cell in which a prisoner ecstatically dances a Parisian *java*. Simultaneously, the prisoner in the next cell (the homosexual lover of the first prisoner, it turns out) paces for a short time, stops, and taps on the wall to his lover, who is still dancing. The first prisoner, hearing the knock, smiles and looks at the tatoo of a human head on his chest, which he caresses. The second prisoner, with tears in his eyes, kisses the wall while the first caresses his tatoo. Eventually, the homosexual lover lights a cigarette, forces a tube through a small hole in the wall, and blows smoke through it into the first cell, where the first prisoner continues to dance. Now the second prisoner chews a piece of bread and pushes bits of the masticated bread through the hole, after which he lies on his cot to masturbate.

At this point, the prison guard, a voyeur, appears and looks into a number of cells where prisoners are engaged in explicitly photographed acts of onanism. Finally, the guard arrives at the cell of the first prisoner, who removes one of his socks and caresses his chest. When the second prisoner knocks on the wall, the guard goes to the other cell and peers into it to see the homosexual kissing the wall. The first prisoner takes a straw and pushes it through the wall to the second, who now lights another cigarette, blowing the smoke through the straw to the first prisoner. The film now cuts back to the opening image of hands and flower garland, and we see two lovers passionately embracing. The camera, at this point, flashes to the guard, who takes out his revolver, removes his belt from his trousers, enters the cell of the second homosexual, and beats him sadistically. The prisoner smiles sadly and kneels.

In the flashback (or dream sequence) that follows, we are confronted with the two prisoners in a country meadow. The first caresses a garland of flowers (the same as in the opening sequence), which covers his genital area. The two play racing games in the field for a while before the first prisoner presents a flower from the garland to the second. The next image repeats the motif of the swinging garland presented in the opening sequence of the film. In rapid succession, we are shown a profusion of filmic images. Two male lovers caress; two mouths exude flames; the second prisoner lies on his cot while the guard stands over him.

Then, in another flashback, the second prisoner sniffs the flower earlier presented to him, picks up the first prisoner, carries him to a grassy spot, places him on it, and undoes his trousers. The film next flashes forward to a view of the second prisoner on the cot and to still another view of the swinging garland. At this point, explicit dream sequences of fellatio and sodomy are flashed on the screen, making these acts look more like writhing agony than breathless pleasure.

The film next returns to the prison cell with the second prisoner and the guard. The guard takes his revolver and jams it rather forcefully into the prisoner's mouth, at which juncture both their faces take on a look of ecstasy. And the camera now presents yet another image of the flower garland. The second prisoner, in his cell, knocks on the wall, but he receives no response from the first prisoner. The camera pans the prison yard as the guard walks away, and we are presented with a last view of the swinging garland, which is finally caught by the empty hand. The last frames of the film catch the inscription "*Juin 1950*" on the brick wall before the fade out.

Such a short description of the film invariably enhances its more grotesque aspects in the telling—and it does contain grotesqueries. The viewer is hard put, for instance, to suppress embarrassed chuckles during the scene involving the guard, the prisoner, and the revolver toward the end of the film; it verges on amateurish, inept parody of Freudian dream symbolism.

Moreover, the maudlin aspect of the sequences in which the homosexual prisoner, with tears in his eyes, caresses the wall amuses the viewer, and it shouldn't; it seems overdone to the point of burlesque. Notwithstanding these major defects, however, there are flashes of pure cinematic genius in the film. At times, for example, Genet employs the camera in such a way as to capture the kind of misty, lyrical beauty that Jean Renoir caught in his films. And his insistent scattershot repetition of the flower imagery brings to mind the kind of image repetition that D. W. Griffith revelled in. But his most formidable technical accomplishment is the rapid, jarring juxtaposition of images that presages the techniques employed by Jean-Luc Godard, François Truffaut, and Richard Lester in such films as *Weekend*, *Jules et Jim*, and *A Hard Day's Night*.

Most of all, however, the film elucidates the world of the prisoner, a world that is, for the early Genet, suffused in the soft, hazy light of play. Genet, the ex-prisoner, produces out of the play of his imagination a wordless fantasy about prisoners whose only hope is the playful world of illusion. If it sounds familiar, we have only to look at *Deathwatch* and *The Maids* to discover where the ideas originate.

 **NOTES**

Introduction

1 Sigmund Freud, *Civilization and Its Discontents*, trans. Jas. Strachey (New York, 1961), p. 27.

2 Johan Huizinga, *Homo Ludens* (Boston, 1950), p. 14.

3 Herbert Marcuse, *Eros and Civilization* (New York, 1955), p. 171.

4 (New York, 1963), p. 169.

5 Antonin Artaud, *The Theater and Its Double*, trans. M.C. Richards (New York, 1958), p. 53.

6 Artaud, p. 82.

Chapter i

1 Jean-Paul Sartre, *Saint Genet, comédien et martyr* (Paris, 1952), p. 9. The French text, in each case, appears in these notes.

Un enfant meurt de honte, surgit à sa place un voyou; le voyou sera hanté par l'enfant. Il faudrait parler de résurrection, évoquer les vieux rites initiatiques du chamanisme et des sociétés secrètes si Genet ne refusait catégoriquement d'être un ressuscité. Il y a eu mort, c'est tout. Et Genet n'est rien d'autre qu'un mort.

2 Tom Driver, *Jean Genet* (New York, 1966), p. 15.

3 Ibid., p. 32.

4 "Playboy Interview: Jean Genet," *Playboy* 10 (April 1964), 46.

5 Ibid.

6 Jean Genet, *Miracle de la Rose*, in *Oeuvres Complètes de Jean Genet* 2 (Paris, 1951), p. 195.

Par Harcamone, Divers et Bulkaen, je vais encore revivre Mettray qui fut mon enfance. Je vais retrouver la Colonie pénitentiaire abolie, le bagne d'enfants détruit.

7 Ibid., p. 395.

Harcamone est mort, Bulkaen est mort. Si je sors, comme après la mort de Pilorge, j'irai fouiller les vieux journaux. Comme de Pilorge, il ne restera plus entre les mains qu'un article très bref, sur un mauvais papier, une sorte de cendre grise qui m'apprendra qu'il fut exécuté à l'aube. Ces papiers sont leur tombeau. Mais je me transmettrai très loin dans le temps leur nom. Ce nom, seul, restera dans le futur débarrassé de son objet. Qui étaient Bulkaen, Harcamone, Divers, qui était Pilorge, qui était Guy? demandera-t-on. Et leur nom troublera comme la lumière nous trouble qui arrive d'une étoile morte il y a mille ans. Ài-je dit tout ce qu'il fallait dire de cette aventure? Si je quitte ce livre, je quitte ce qui peut se raconter. Le reste est indicible. Je me tais et marche les pieds nus.

8 Jean Genet, *Journal du voleur* (Paris, 1949), p. 132.

Pas plus que moi-même Stilitano n'était vraiment un homme mur. . . . il jouait au gangster, c'est-à-dire qu'il en inventait les attitudes. Je ne connais pas de voyous qui ne soient des enfants. Quel esprit «sérieux», s'il passe devant une bijouterie, une banque, inventerait minutieusement et gravement, les détails d'une attaque ou d'un cambriolage? . . . Stilitano jouait. Il aimait se savoir hors la loi, se sentir en danger. . . . Il tentait de copier un héros idéal, le Stilitano dont l'image était déjà inscrite dans un ciel de gloire.

CHAPTER 2

1 Although a French text of *Haute Surveillance* exists (Paris: Gallimard, 1949), Genet made many changes in that text when the play was produced on the stage. The English translation by Bernard Frechtman (New York: Grove Press, 1961) follows the revised *acting edition* of the play—which, curiously, is not as yet in print in French.

2 Sartre, *Saint Genet*, p. 33.
«Nul ne fait le mal volontairement.» Bien sûr: qu'y gagnerait-on? Le mal est gratuit; c'est une activité de luxe qui demande des loisirs et ne rapporte rien. «Le crime ne paie pas», disent-ils. Et ils ont raison: le Mal, comme le Bien, exige d'être à lui-même sa propre récompense.

3 Jean Genet, *The Maids and Deathwatch*, trans. Bernard Frechtman (New York, 1961), pp. 161–62.
4 Ibid., pp. 147–48.
5 Ibid., p. 145.
6 Ibid., pp. 135–36.
7 Ibid., p. 103.
8 Ibid., p. 104.
9 Ibid., p. 103.
10 Ibid., pp. 103–4.
11 Ibid., pp. 139–40.
12 Ibid., pp. 141–42.

13 Although Genet wrote *Deathwatch* first, it was presented on the stage after *The Maids.*

Page references at the end of each passage quoted hereinafter in the body of the text refer to Grove Press editions of the dramas translated by Bernard Frechtman. Page references in these notes refer to the French editions.

14 Jean Genet, *Les Bonnes* (Décines, 1963), p. 13.

> La chambre de Madame. Meubles Louis XV. Dentelles. Au fond, une fenêtre ouverte sur la façade de l'immeuble en face. À droite, le lit. . . . Des fleurs à profusion. C'est le soir.

15 Jules Michelet, *Satanism and Witchcraft*, trans. A.R. Allinson (New York, 1939), chapters 11, 12, and 13.

16 David Grossvogel, *Brecht, Ionesco, Beckett, Genet: Four Playwrights and a Postscript* (Ithaca, 1962), p. 147.

17 J. Jacobsen and Wm. R. Mueller, *Ionesco and Genet: Playwrights of Silence* (New York, 1968), p. 145.

CHAPTER 3

1 Jean Genet, *Le Balcon* (Décines, 1961), p. 7.

> Les sentiments des protagonistes, inspirés par la situation, sont-ils feints, sont-ils réels? La colère, vers la fin de la pièce, du Chef de la Police à l'égard des Trois Figures, est-elle feinte, est-elle réelle? L'existence des révoltés est dans le bordel, ou au dehors? Il faut tenir l'équivoque jusqu'à la fin.

2 Ibid, p. 11.

> Sur la paroi de droite un miroir—dont le cadre est doré et sculpté— reflète un lit défait qui, si la pièce était disposée logiquement, se trouverait dans la salle, aux premiers fauteuils d'orchestre. (English from *The Balcony*, unrevised edition, © 1960 by Bernard Frechtman.)

3 Ibid., pp. 204–5.

> Tout à l'heure, il va falloir recommencer . . . tout rallumer . . . s'habiller. . . . (Elle s'arrête au milieu de la scène, face au public.) . . . il faut rentrer chez vous, où tout, n'en doutez pas, sera encore plus faux qu'ici. . . . Il faut vous en aller. . . . Vous passerez à droite, par la ruelle. . . . (Elle éteint une dernière lumière.) C'est déjà le matin.

4 Genet is to use screens again in another drama with such effect that he named the drama in which they occur *The Screens.*

5 Genet, *Le Balcon*, p. 58.

> C'est une chambre dont les trois panneaux visibles sont trois miroirs où se reflète un petit vieux vêtu en clochard. . . .

Tous les gestes du petit vieux se reflètent dans les trois miroirs. (Il faut donc trois acteurs tenant les rôles de reflets.)

6 Ibid., p. 63.

Je n'accorde pas qu'on blague. . . . S'il y a sourire, il y a doute. Les clients veulent des cérémonies graves. Avec soupirs. Ma maison est un lieu sévère.

7 Robert Brustein, *The Theatre of Revolt* (Boston, 1964), p.379.
8 Genet becomes interested, as a matter of fact, in the perversion of the Roman Catholic Mass encountered in the Black Mass.
9 Huizinga, *Homo Ludens*, chapter 1.
10 Genet, *Le Balcon*, p. 30.

Le Juge: . . . Écoute: il faut que tu sois une voleuse modèle, si tu veux que je sois un juge modèle. Fausse voleuse, je deviens un faux juge. C'est clair?
La Voleuse: Oh oui, monsieur le Juge.
Le Juge (il continue à lire): Bien. Jusqu'à présent tout se passait bien. Mon bourreau cognait dur . . . car lui aussi a sa fonction. Nous sommes liés; toi, lui, moi. Par exemple, s'il ne cognait pas, comment pourrais-je l'arrêter de cogner? Donc, il doit frapper pour que j'intervienne et prouve mon autorité. Et tu dois nier afin qu'il te frappe.

11 Ibid., p. 8.

Il va de soi que le costume d'Irma doit être, au début de la pièce, très austère. On peut même la supposer en deuil. C'est dans la scène avec Carmen qu'elle s'attifera, portera cette robe longue qui, dans la scène du Balcon deviendra, grâce à quelques décorations, la robe de la Reine.

12 Ibid., pp. 65–66.

Irma [speaking of her whores]: Comment vous nommerai-je, mes grandes, mes longues stériles? Ils ne vous fécondent jamais, et pourtant. . . si vous n'étiez pas là?

13 Grossvogel, *Four Playwrights*, p. 163.
14 Genet, *Le Balcon*, p. 118.

Roger: Tu es à moi. Je t'ai . . .
Chantal (agacée): Je sais: tirée d'un tombeau.

15 Ibid., p. 170–71.

L'Évêque: Alors, nous rentrons dans nos chambres y poursuivre la recherche d'une dignité absolue. Nous y étions bien et c'est vous qui êtes venu pour nous en tirer. . . . De cet état adorable, sans malheur, vous nous avez tirés brutalement.
Le Général (interrompant l'Évêque): Ma culotte! Quand j'enfilais ma culotte, quel bonheur! À présent, je dors avec ma culotte de général, je

mange avec ma culotte, . . . je vis dans ma culotte de général. Je suis général comme on est évêque!

. . . .

. . . autrefois c'était un mois à l'avance!—me préparer à enfiler ma culotte ni mes bottes de général. Je les ai, pour l'éternité, autour des pattes. Je ne rêve plus, ma parole.

L'Évêque (au Chef de la Police): Vous voyez, il ne rêve plus. La pureté ornementale, notre luxueuse et stérile—et sublime—apparence est rongée.

16 Martin Esslin, *The Theatre of the Absurd* (New York, 1961), p. 158.

17 Lionel Abel, *Metatheatre* (New York, 1963), p. 82.

18 Brustein, p. 401.

19 Ibid.

20 Georges Bataille, *Death and Sensuality* (New York, 1962), p. 14.

21 Ibid., p. 59.

22 Norman O. Brown, *Life Against Death* (New York, 1959), p. 131.

23 Ibid., p. 29.

CHAPTER 4

1 It is interesting to note the similarity of these figures to the Queen, the Envoy, the Bishop, the Judge, and the General in *The Balcony*.

2 In "Pour Jouer *Les Nègres*," which introduces the Arbalète edition of the play (Décines: Arbalète, 1960), Genet indicates Roger Blin's use of music and dance in the original Paris production as better than his own, and he states his preference for Blin's ending:

> Voici comment Roger Blin terminait la pièce: à peine Vertu et Village ont échangé leur dernière réplique que tous les acteurs rentrent en scène et se mettent à danser sur un rythme africain. Ville de Saint-Nazaire en profite pour passer en coulisse. Soudain, à la musique africaine succèdent les premières mesures du menuet de Mozart. C'est alors que Ville de Saint-Nazaire apparaît . . . il porte à bout de bras le catafalque blanc couvert de fleurs . . . il pose le catafalque où il doit se trouver au début de la pièce, puis, la musique n'ayant pas cessé, tous se mettent à danser le menuet de Mozart. Rideau. Cette façon d'achever la pièce a ma préférence.
>
> (Here is the way Roger Blin ended the play: scarcely have Virtue and Village ended their final dialogue when all the actors reenter onstage and begin to dance to an African rhythm. Ville de Saint-Nazaire disappears into the wings. Suddenly, the first measures of the Mozart minuet succeed the African music. It's then Saint-Nazaire appears . . . he carries at the end of his arms the white catafalque covered with flowers . . . he places the catafalque where it should be found at the beginning of the play; then, the music not having stopped, everyone starts to dance the Mozart minuet. Curtain.
>
> This way of achieving the drama has my preference.)

3 Jean Genet, *Les Nègres* (Décines, 1960), p. 13.

Cette pièce . . . est destinée à un public de Blancs. Mais si, par improbable, elle était jouée un soir devant un public de Noirs, il faudrait qu'à chaque représentation un Blanc fût invité. . . . L'organisateur du Spectacle ira le recevoir solennellement, le fera habiller d'un costume de cérémonie et le conduira à sa place, de préférence au centre de la première rangée des fauteuils d'orchestre. On jouera pour lui. Sur ce Blanc symbolique un projecteur sera dirigé durant tout le spectacle.

4 Ibid., p. 17.
5 Genet, *Les Nègres*, p. 16.

Chaque acteur en sera un Noir masqué dont le masque est un visage de Blanc posé de telle façon qu'on voie une large bande noire autour, et même les cheveux crépus.

6 Ibid., p. 24.

Archibald: Quittée cette scène, nous sommes mêlés à votre vie: je suis cuisinier, madame est lingère, monsieur étudie la médecine, monsieur est vicaire à Sainte-Clotilde, madame . . . passons. Ce soir, nous ne songerons qu'à vous divertir. . . .

7 Ibid., p. 178.

Comme j'ai aimé. Et maintenant, je meurs, faut-il l'avouer, étouffée par mon désir d'un Grand Nègre qui me tue. Nudité noir, tu m'as vaincue.

8 Ibid., pp. 179–80.

La Reine (tournée vers les Nègres): Adieu, et bonne chance. Bonne fille, je souhaite que tout aille bien pour vous. . . . nous avons vécu longtemps, nous allons. . . . nous resterons engourdis dans la Terre comme des larves ou des taupes, et si un jour . . . dans dix mille ans. . . .

9 Huizinga, *Homo Ludens*, p. 26.
10 Norman O. Brown, trans., *Hesiod's Theogony* (New York, 1953), pp. 17–18.
11 Genet, *Les Nègres*, p. 58.

Village: J'aime Vertu. Elle m'aime.
Archibald: Elle, oui, peut-être. Elle a plus de pouvoirs que toi. . . . Elle peut . . . t'apporter ce qui ressemble le plus à l'amour: la tendresse. Dans ses bras, tu seras son gosse, pas son amant.

12 Ibid., pp. 53–55.

Village: . . . Quand je vous vis . . . je crois, durant une seconde, la force de nier tout ce qui n'était pas vous, et de rire devant l'illusion, hélas mes épaules sont bien fragiles. Je ne pus supporter la condamnation du monde. Et je me suis mis à vous haïr quand tout en vous m'eût fait entrevoir l'amour, et que l'amour m'eût rendu insupportable le mépris des hommes, et ce mépris insupportable mon amour pour vous. Exactement, je vous hais.

. . . .

Village (qui avait baissé la tête, la relève pour reprendre son récit) : . . . Je ne sais pas si vous êtes belle—j'ai peur que vous ne le soyez. J'ai peur de la ténèbre, crépitante d'étincelles, que vous êtes ! Ténèbre, mère auguste de ma Race, Ombre, tunique exacte qui me gante de l'orteil à la paupière, long sommeil où le plus fragile de vos enfants voudrait s'enrouler, je ne sais pas si vous êtes belle, mais vous êtes l'Afrique, ô Nuit monumentale, et je vous hais . . . de remplir de douceur mes yeux noirs . . . de m'obliger à ce dur travail qui consiste à vous écarter de moi, à vous haïr. Il suffirait de peu de chose pour que me réjouissent votre visage, votre corps, vos mouvements, votre coeur . . .

Archibald: Prenez garde, Village !

Village (à Vertu): Mais je vous hais !

13 Marcuse, *Eros and Civilization*, p. 68.
14 Genet, *Les Nègres*, p. 62.

Le Juge: La Reine est endormie (un doigt sur sa bouche). Elle couve. Quoi? Les verrières de Chartres et les vestiges celtiques.

Le Gouverneur: Qu'on la réveille, nom de Dieu . . . le coup de la gamelle comme à la caserne . . .

Le Juge: Vous êtes fou ! Et qui va couver? Vous?

15 "Au théâtre de Lutèce, [Roger] Blin—et il a eu raison—a ordonné les comédiens de telle façon que Vertu vienne se placer juste au-dessous de la Reine." [Note on p. 64 of *Les Nègres*]

(At the Lutece Theatre, Roger Blin—and he was right—ordered the actors in such a fashion that Virtue has just been placed directly below the Queen.)

16 Genet, *Les Nègres*, pp. 64–65.

Vertu (doucement, comme somnambulique) : Je suis la Reine Occidentale à la pâleur de lys ! Résultat précieux de tant de siècles travaillés pour un pareil miracle ! Immaculée douce à l'oeil et à l'âme ! . . .(Toute la Cour écoute, attentive.) . . . je suis blanche. Si la mort me fixe, c'est dans la couleur de victoire. O nobles pâleurs, colorez mes tempes, mes doigts, mon ventre ! Oeil, iris aux nuances délicates . . . gazon anglais, gazon normand, par vous, mais que voit-on? . . . (La Reine qui s'est enfin réveillée, stupéfaite, écoute le poème, puis elle va réciter en même temps que Vertu.) . . . Blanche, c'est le lait qui m'indique, c'est le lys, la colombe. . . .

. . . .

Vertu et la Reine (ensemble): . . . Sauf qu'un peu d'ombre est restée sous mon aisselle. . . .

17 Ibid., pp. 65 and 69.

Vertu (seule): ... un cerne bistre, violet, presque noir, gagne ma joue. La nuit. ...

. . . .

La Reine (soudain éveillée): Assez! Et faites-les taire, ils ont volé ma voix! Au secours ...

(Soudain, Félicité se lève. Tout le monde la regarde, se tait, et l'écoute.)
Félicité: Dahomey! ... Dahomey! ... À mon secours, Nègres de tous les coins du monde. Venez! ... Entrez en moi, multitude, et soyez, pour ce soir, seulement, ma force et ma raison.

18 Ibid., p. 74.

(... tous tournent la tête: Madame Félicité descend de son trône, très majestueuse. Elle s'approche du catafalque, se baisse, et sous le drap passe quelques graines.)
Bobo: Déjà!
Félicité: Je ne la gave pas, vous savez. Pourtant, il vaut mieux qu'elle ne dépérisse pas.
Diouf: Et qu'est-ce qu'elle mange? Du riz?
Félicité: Du blé.

19 H.R. Hays, *In the Beginnings* (New York, 1963), p. 109.

20 Genet, *Les Nègres*, p. 154.
... la Nuit en personne. Non celle qui est absence de lumière, mais la mère généreuse et terrible qui contient la lumière et les actes.

21 Ibid., pp. 146 and 151.

Personne n'aurait la force de le nier. Il pousse, il pousse, ma belle, il grandit, verdit, il éclate en corolles, en parfums, et c'est toute l'Afrique ce bel arbre, mon crime!

22 Mircea Eliade, *Patterns in Comparative Religion* (London, 1958), p. 182.
23 This is the "Lettre de l'Auteur" that introduces the two versions of *Les Bonnes* published in one volume by J. J. Pauvert (Sceaux, 1954).
24 Genet, *Les Nègres*, pp. 152–53.

Félicité: Si vous êtes la lumière et que nous soyons l'ombre, tant qu'il y aura la nuit où vient sombrer le jour ...
La Reine: Je vais vous faire exterminer.
Félicité (ironique): Sotte, que vous seriez plate, sans cette ombre qui vous donne tant de relief.

25 Ibid., p. 152.

Les deux femmes avancent côte à côte ... presque amicalement.

26 Ibid., p. 156.

[La Reine] et Félicité vont se parler comme deux femmes échangeant des recettes de ménagère.

27 Joseph Campbell, *The Hero with a Thousand Faces* (Cleveland, 1949), p. 115.

28 Huizinga, p. 164.

29 Marcuse, p. 58.

CHAPTER 5

1 Jean Genet, *Letters to Roger Blin: Reflections on the Theater*, trans. Richard Seaver (New York, 1969), p. 14.

2 Jean Genet, *Les Paravents* (Décines, 1961), p. 260.

> Pendant les deux ou trois dernières répliques, les morts déjà emportaient leurs paravents. La Mère sort la dernière, avec son fauteuil. La scène est vide. C'est fini.

3 Jacobsen and Mueller, *Ionesco and Genet*, p. 209.

4 Although the director Blin finally presented *The Screens* indoors, Genet was delighted with the results. He wrote to Blin:

> In *The Screens*, the full credit goes to you. If I had thought that the play could be performed, I would have made it more beautiful—or a complete failure. Without touching it, you have taken it and made it light. It's very beautiful. You have my friendship, and my admiration (Genet, *Letters*, p. 41).

5 Genet, *Les Paravents*, p. 9.

> Voici comment cette pièce doit être montée: dans un théâtre en plein air. Une sorte de terre-plein rectangulaire, clos d'une très haute palissade de planches. . . . Le fond et les côtés de la scène seront constitués par de hautes planches inégales, et noires. Elles seront disposées de telle facon . . . que des plates-formes, à différentes hauteurs, pourront sortir de droite et de gauche. De sorte qu'on possédera un jeu très varié de scènes, de niveaux et de surfaces différents. Par les espaces ménagés entre les planches de droite et de gauche, apparaîtront et sortiront les paravents et les comédiens.

6 See passage below quoted from Genet's directions concerning make-up.

7 Ibid., p. 10.

Les Personnages

> Si possible, ils seront masqués. Sinon, très maquillés, très fardés (même les soldats). Maquillages excessifs contrastant avec le réalisme des costumes. Le mieux serait de prévoir une grande variété de nez postiches. . . . Aucun visage ne devra garder cette beauté conventionnelle des traits dont on joue trop au théâtre comme au cinéma.

8 Genet refused permission to a famous Polish theatrical company that desired to present *The Blacks* with white actors made up as blacks.

9 Genet, *Les Paravents*, p. 10.

Auprès du paravent, il devra toujours y avoir au moins un objet réel
(brouette, seau, bicyclette, etc.), destiné à confronter sa propre réalité avec
les objets dessinés.

10 Ibid., p. 92.

> *Sir Harold* (courroucé) : . . . Je ne suis plus le patron?
> *Malik* : Oh yes! Oh yes, Sir Harold. Vous êtes notre père. Dommage
> qu'on ne soit pas vos enfants.

11 Ibid., p. 22.

> *Warda* : . . . Quand le soleil est tombé je ne pourrais rien faire sans mes
> parures . . . même écarter les jambes pour pisser je ne pourrais pas, mais
> juponnée d'or, je suis la Reine des Averses.

12 Ibid., p. 24.

> *Malika* : N'importe qui n'approche pas de nos cuisses. On doit frapper
> avant d'entrer.
> *Warda* (hautaine, même voix traînante, désenchantée) : Vingt-quatre
> ans ! . . . Une putain ça ne s'improvise pas, ça se murit. J'ai mis vingt-quatre
> ans. Et je suis douée! Un homme, qu'est-ce que c'est? Un homme reste
> un homme. Devant nous c'est lui qui se met nu comme une putain de
> Toul ou de Nancy.

13 Ibid., pp. 180–81.

> *Warda* : Où est le temps, miroir, où je pouvais me regarder des heures
> en bâillant? (Elle crache sur le miroir.) Où sont les hommes qui me regar-
> daient me regarder sans même oser respirer? Maintenant on est au boulot. Et
> répondre bonjour aux femmes qu'on rencontre chez l'épicier, c'est moins re-
> posant que je n'aurais cru. . . .
>
> . . . .
>
> Il y avait loin, il y avait un Sahara, entre moi Warda et la femme la plus
> méprisée du village, entre moi et Leïla. Un chef de bataillon de l'artillerie
> coloniale—je te parle d'il y a un an—était venu une après-midi et il fallait
> lui recoudre trois boutons : c'est lui avec ses gros doigts bagués, qui a rac-
> commodé sa braguette, moi je ne savais pas. Aujourd'hui si. Sucer le fil,
> enfiler l'aiguille. . . . À la boucherie, à l'épicerie on me dit bonjour. . . .
> Je suis de moins en moins quelqu'un. . . . Et ma colère est de plus en plus
> grande et ma tristesse aussi.

14 Marcuse, *Eros and Civilization*, pp. ix–x.
15 Genet, *Les Paravents*, pp. 253 and 255.

> *Ommou* (au combattant) : On n'a rien à faire avec toi, tu raisonnes.
> *Le Combattant* : Si on veut s'organiser, il faut raisonner. Nous les combat-
> tants, on a droit à quoi?
>
> . . . .

D'ici peu nous serons . . . cartésiens.

16 Brown, *Life Against Death*, p. 293.

17 Ibid., p. 191.

18 Genet, *Les Paravents*, p. 260.

> *La Mère* (inquiète): Et Saïd? Il vient?
>
> . . . .
>
> *La Mère:* Saïd! . . . Il n'y a plus qu'à l'attendre . . .
>
> *Kadidja* (riant): Pas la peine. Pas plus que Leïla, il ne reviendra pas.

19 Freud, *Civilization and Its Discontents*, p. 71.

Conclusion

1 Joseph McMahon, *The Imagination of Jean Genet* (New Haven, 1963), p. 242.

2 Genet, *Letters*, pp. 62–63.

3 Campbell, *Hero*, p. 115.

4 Genet, *Letters*, pp. 19–20.

5 Ibid., p. 14.

Appendix

1 Although *The Balcony* was made into a film, Genet had nothing to do with its filming. The film, as a matter of fact, is quite different from the play. He did, however, write the story for the film *Mademoiselle*, but again he had little to do with the actual filming of the story.

2 The film has no evident connection with the author's poem of the same name—except, perhaps, the fact that it deals with criminals.

SELECTED BIBLIOGRAPHY

Note: According to the latest information, a complete edition of all of Genet's drama is now in preparation by Gallimard of Paris.

JEAN GENET

Nondramatic works

Journal du voleur. Paris: Gallimard, 1949.

L'Atelier d'Alberto Giacometti. Décines: Arbalète, 1963.

Letters to Roger Blin: Reflections on the Theater. Translated by Richard Seaver. New York: Grove Press, 1969.

Miracle de la Rose (ed. originale reliée). Décines: Arbalète, 1946.

Miracle de la Rose. Décines: Arbalète, 1956.

Miracle of the Rose. Translated by Bernard Frechtman. New York: Grove Press, 1966.

Notre-Dame-des-Fleurs. Décines: Arbalète, 1948.

★ *Oeuvres Complètes de Jean Genet,* vol. 2 (comprising *Notre-Dame-des-Fleurs,* "Le Condamné a Mort," *Miracle de la Rose,* and "Un Chant d'amour"). Paris: Gallimard, 1951.

★ *Oeuvres Complètes de Jean Genet,* vol. 3 (comprising *Pompes funèbres,* "Le Pêcheur du Suquet," and *Querelle de Brest*). Paris: Gallimard, 1953.

Our Lady of the Flowers. Translated by Bernard Frechtman. New York: Bantam Books, 1963.

Poèmes. Décines: Arbalète, 1948.

Poèmes. Décines: Arbalète, 1962.

"The Members of the Assembly." Translated by Richard Seaver. *Esquire* 70 (November 1968), 86–89.

The Thief's Journal. Translated by Bernard Frechtman. New York: Bantam Books, 1964.

Dramatic works

Haute Surveillance. Paris: Gallimard, 1949.

Le Balcon (avec un avertissement). Décines: Arbalète, 1960.

Le Balcon (édition définitive précédée de «Comment jouer le Balcon»). Décines: Arbalète, 1962.

Les Bonnes (Les deux versions précédées d'une Lettre de l'Auteur). Sceaux: J. J. Pauvert, 1954.

Les Bonnes (et "Comment jouer les Bonnes"). Décines: Arbalète, 1963.

Les Nègres. Décines: Arbalète, 1960.

Les Nègres (précédée de "Pour jouer les Nègres"). Décines: Arbalète, 1963.

Les Paravents. Décines: Arbalète, 1961.

The Balcony. Translated by Bernard Frechtman. New York: Grove Press, 1960.

The Balcony: Revised Edition. Translated by Bernard Frechtman. New York: Grove Press, 1966.

The Blacks. Translated by Bernard Frechtman. New York: Grove Press, 1960.

The Maids and Deathwatch. Translated by Bernard Frechtman. New York: Grove Press, 1961.

The Screens. Translated by Bernard Frechtman. New York: Grove Press, 1962.

* Volume I of the *Oeuvres Complètes de Jean Genet* is Jean-Paul Sartre's *Saint Genet, comédien et martyr* (q.v.).

SECONDARY SOURCES

Abel, Lionel. *Metatheatre.* New York: Hill & Wang, 1963, pp. 76–83.

Artaud, Antonin. *The Theater and Its Double.* Translated by Mary Caroline Richards. New York: Grove Press, 1958.

Barish, Jonas A. "The Veritable Saint Genet." *Wisconsin Studies in Contemporary Literature* 7 (Autumn 1965), 267–85.

Barr, Stringfellow. *The Will of Zeus.* Philadelphia: J. B. Lippincott Company, 1962.

Bataille, Georges. *Death and Sensuality.* New York: Walker and Company, 1962.

————. *La Littérature et le Mal.* Paris: Gallimard, 1957, pp. 185–226.

————. *L'Erotisme.* Paris: Minuit, 1957.

Beigbeder, Marc. *Le Théâtre en France depuis la Libération.* Paris: Bordas, 1959, pp. 158–60.

Birket-Smith, Kaj. *Paths of Culture.* Translated by Darin Fennow. Madison: University of Wisconsin Press, 1965.

Brecht, Bertolt. *Seven Plays.* Edited by Eric Bentley. New York: Grove Press, 1961.

Brown, Norman O. *Hesiod's Theogony.* New York: The Liberal Arts Press, 1953.

————. *Life Against Death.* New York: Vintage Books, 1959.

————. *Love's Body.* New York: Random House, 1966.

Brustein, Robert. *The Theatre of Revolt.* Boston: Little, Brown and Co., 1964, pp. 361–411.

Campbell, Joseph. *The Hero with a Thousand Faces.* Cleveland: Meridan Books, 1949.

Cetta, Lewis T. "Jean Genet as Guru: A Note on the Ending of *The Screens.*" *Notes on Contemporary Literature* 1 (May 1971), 11–13.

————. "Jean Genet as *Homo Ludens* in Quest of Profane Play." *Connecticut Review* 6 (October 1972), 26–33.

————. "Myth, Magic, and Play in Genet's *The Blacks.*" *Contemporary Literature* 11 (Autumn 1970), 511–525.

Cismaru, Alfred. "The Antitheism of Jean Genet." *Antioch Review* 24 (Fall 1964), 387–401.

Clark, Eleanor. "The World of Jean Genet." *Partisan Review* 16 (April 1949), 442–48.

Codignola, Luciano. "Jean Genet, o l'illusione dello scandalo." *Tempo Presente* 2 (September-October 1957), 773–75.

Coe, Richard. *The Vision of Jean Genet.* New York: Grove Press, 1968.

Cruickshank, John. "Jean Genet: The Aesthetics of Crime." *Critical Quarterly* 6 (Autumn 1964), 202–10.

Dance in India, The. New Delhi: Publications Division, Ministry of Information and Broadcasting, Govt. of India, 1964.

Dort, Bernard. "Le Jeu de Genet." *Les Temps Modernes* 15 (June 1960), 1875–84.

Driver, Tom. *Jean Genet.* New York: Columbia University Press, 1966.

————. "Spiritual Diabolism of Jean Genet." *Christian Century* 80 (November 20, 1963), 1433–35.

Duvignaud, Jean. "Roger Blin aux prises avec *Les Nègres de Genet*." *Les Lettres Nouvelles*, October 28, 1959, pp. 24–26.

Eliade, Mircea. *Myth and Reality*. New York: Harper and Row, 1963.

———. *Patterns in Comparative Religion*. London: Sheed and Ward, 1958.

Elson, J. "Genet and the Sadistic Society." *London Magazine*, August 1963, pp. 61–67.

Erikson, Erik H. *Childhood and Society*. New York: W.W.Norton & Co., 1963.

Esslin, Martin. *Brecht: The Man and His Work*. New York: Anchor Books, 1961.

———. *The Theatre of the Absurd*. New York: Anchor Books, 1961.

Fowlie, Wallace. *Dionysus in Paris*. New York: Meridian Books, 1958, pp. 218–22.

———. "The Case of Jean Genet." *Commonweal* 73 (October 28, 1960), 111–13.

Freud, Sigmund. *The Complete Psychological Works of Sigmund Freud*. Edited and translated by James Strachey. London: Hogarth Press, 1964.

———. *Civilization and Its Discontents*. Translated by James Strachey. New York: W.W. Norton & Co., 1961.

Fromm, Erich. *The Forgotten Language: An Introduction to the Understanding of Dreams, Fairy Tales, and Myths*. New York: Rinehart, 1951.

Grossvogel, David. *Brecht, Ionesco, Beckett, Genet: Four Playwrights and a Postscript*. Ithaca: Cornell University Press, 1962, pp. 133–174.

Guicharnaud, Jacques. *Modern French Theatre*. New Haven: Yale University Press, 1961, pp. 168–72.

Harrison, Jane Ellen. *Epilegomena to the Study of Greek Religion* and *Themis* (Reprint in one volume). New Hyde Park: University Books, 1962.

Hays, H.R. *In the Beginnings*. New York: G.P. Putnam's Sons, 1963.

Huizinga, Johan. *Homo Ludens*. Boston: Beacon Press, 1950.

Jacobsen, Josephine, and Mueller, William R. *Ionesco and Genet: Playwrights of Silence*. New York: Hill &Wang, 1968.

Jung, C.G., ed. *Man and His Symbols*. New York: Dell Publishing Co., 1964.

———. *Psyche and Symbol*. Edited by V.S. de Laszlo. New York: Anchor Books, 1958.

Knapp, Bettina. "An Interview with Roger Blin." *Tulane Drama Review* 7 (1963), 111–24.

Lao Tzu. *The Way of Life: Tao Te Ching*. Translated by R.B. Blakney. New York: Mentor Books, 1957.

Lea, Henry C. *Materials Toward a History of Witchcraft*. Edited by Arthur C. Howland. 3 Vols. New York: Thomas Yoseloff, 1939.

Marcuse, Herbert. *Eros and Civilization*. New York: Vintage Books, 1955.

———. *One Dimensional Man*. Boston: Beacon Press, 1964.

McLuhan, Marshall. *The Gutenberg Galaxy*. Toronto: University of Toronto Press, 1962.

———. *The Medium Is the Massage*. New York: Bantam Books, 1967.

———. *Understanding Media*. New York: Signet Books, 1964.

———. *War and Peace in the Global Village*. New York: Bantam Books, 1968.

McMahon, Joseph. *The Imagination of Jean Genet*. New Haven: Yale University Press, 1963.

Michelet, Jules. *Satanism and Witchcraft*. Translated by A.R. Allinson. New York: The Citadel Press, 1939.

Milne, Tom. "Reflections on *The Screens*." *Encore*, no. 50 (July-August 1964), pp. 21–25.

Piaget, Jean. *Play, Dreams, and Imitation in Childhood*. Translated by C. Gattegno and F. M. Hodgson. New York: W. W. Norton & Co., 1962.

"*Playboy* Interview: Jean Genet." *Playboy* 10 (April 1964), 45–53.

Pronko, Leonard. *Avant-Garde: The Experimental Theater in France*. Berkeley: University of California Press, 1964, pp. 140–53.

———. "Jean Genet's *Les Paravents*." *L'Esprit Créatur* (Minneapolis) 2 (Winter 1962), 181–88.

Pucciani, Oreste F. "Tragedy, Genet, and *The Maids.*" *Tulane Drama Review* 7 (Spring 1963), 42–59.

Reck, Rima D. "Appearance and Reality in Genet's *Le Balcon.*" *Yale French Studies*, no. 29 (Spring-Summer 1962), pp. 20–25.

Reich, Wilhelm. *The Discovery of the Orgone.* Translated by Theodore P. Wolfe. New York: Noonday Press, 1961.

Sampurnand, Dr. *The Evolution of the Hindu Pantheon.* Bombay: Bharatiya Vidya Bhavan, 1963.

Sartre, Jean-Paul. *Saint Genet, comédien et martyr* (Vol. 1 of *Oeuvres Complètes de Jean Genet*). Paris: Gallimard, 1952.

———. *Saint Genet.* Translated by Bernard Frechtman. New York: Mentor Books, 1963.

Sellin, Eric. *The Dramatic Concepts of Antonin Artaud.* Chicago: University of Chicago Press, 1968.

Shekhar, I. *Sanskrit Drama: Its Origin and Decline.* Leiden (Netherlands): E.J. Brill, 1960.

Simon, Alfred. "Genet, le nègre et la rèprobation." *Espirit*, no. 280 (January 1960), pp. 170–73.

Smith, Homer. *Man and His Gods.* New York: Grossett and Dunlap, 1952.

Smith, Huston. *The Religions of Man.* New York: Mentor Books, 1958.

Sontag, Susan. *Against Interpretation.* New York: Dell Publishing Co., 1966.

Svendson, J.M. "Corydon Revisited: A Reminder on Genet." *Tulane Drama Review* 7 (Spring 1963), 98–110.

Swander, Homer D. "Shakespeare and the Harlem Clowns: Illusion and Comic Form in Genet's *The Blacks.*" *The Yale Review* 15 (Winter 1966), 209–226.

Taubes, Susan. "The White Mask Falls." *Tulane Drama Review* 7 (Spring 1963), 85–92.

The Upanishads: Breath of the Eternal. Translated by Swami Prabhavananda and F. Manchester. New York: Mentor Books, 1956.

Thody, Phillip. *Jean Genet: A Critical Appraisal.* New York: Stein and Day, 1969.

Weideli, Walter. *The Art of Bertolt Brecht.* Translated by Daniel Russell. New York: New York University Press, 1963.

Wellwarth, George E. *The Theatre of Protest and Paradox.* New York: New York University Press, 1964, pp. 113–33.

Williams, Monier. *Indian Wisdom.* London: William H. Allen and Co., 1875.

Wilson, H.H. *The Religion of the Hindus*, vol. 2. London: Trubner and Company, 1862.

Yeager, H.J. "The Uncompromising Morality of Jean Genet." *French Review* 39 (November 1965), 214–19.

Zadek, Peter. "Acts of Violence." *New Statesman* (May 4, 1957), 568–70.

Zimbardo, R.A. "Genet's Black Mass." *Modern Drama* 8 (December 1965), 247–58.

INDEX